All rights reserved. No part of this publication may be reproduced, stored in a retrieval system or transmitted in form or by any means, electronic, mechanical, photocopy, recording or any other means— except for quotations in printed reviews, without prior permission of the publisher.

ISBN-13: 978-1986089210
ISBN-10: 1986089215

King James Version, Cambridge, 1769. Used by permission. All rights reserved. Copyright © 1982. Used by permission.

All rights reserved.

Published in the United States of America

Copyright ©2018 by Paulette Harper

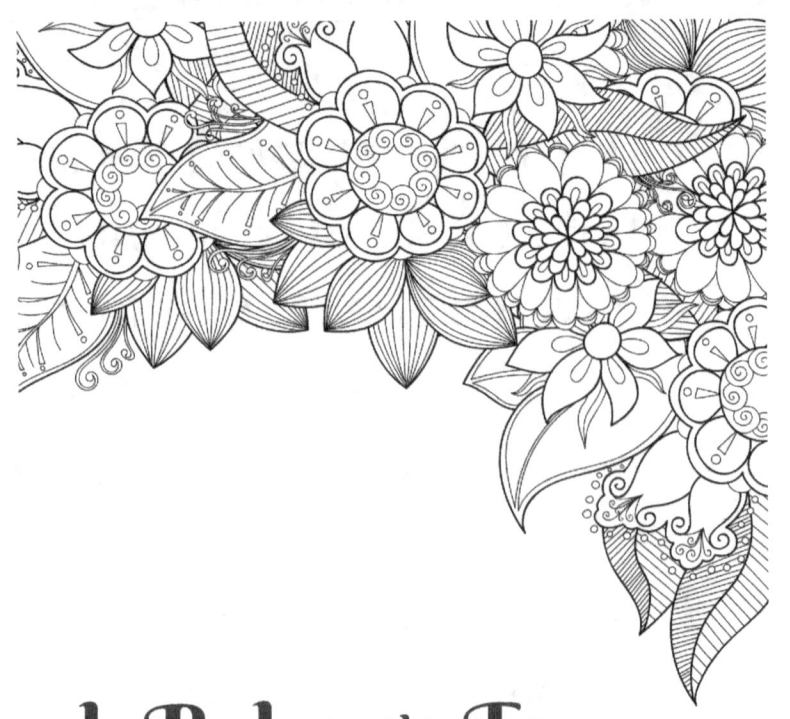

This Book Belongs To

_____

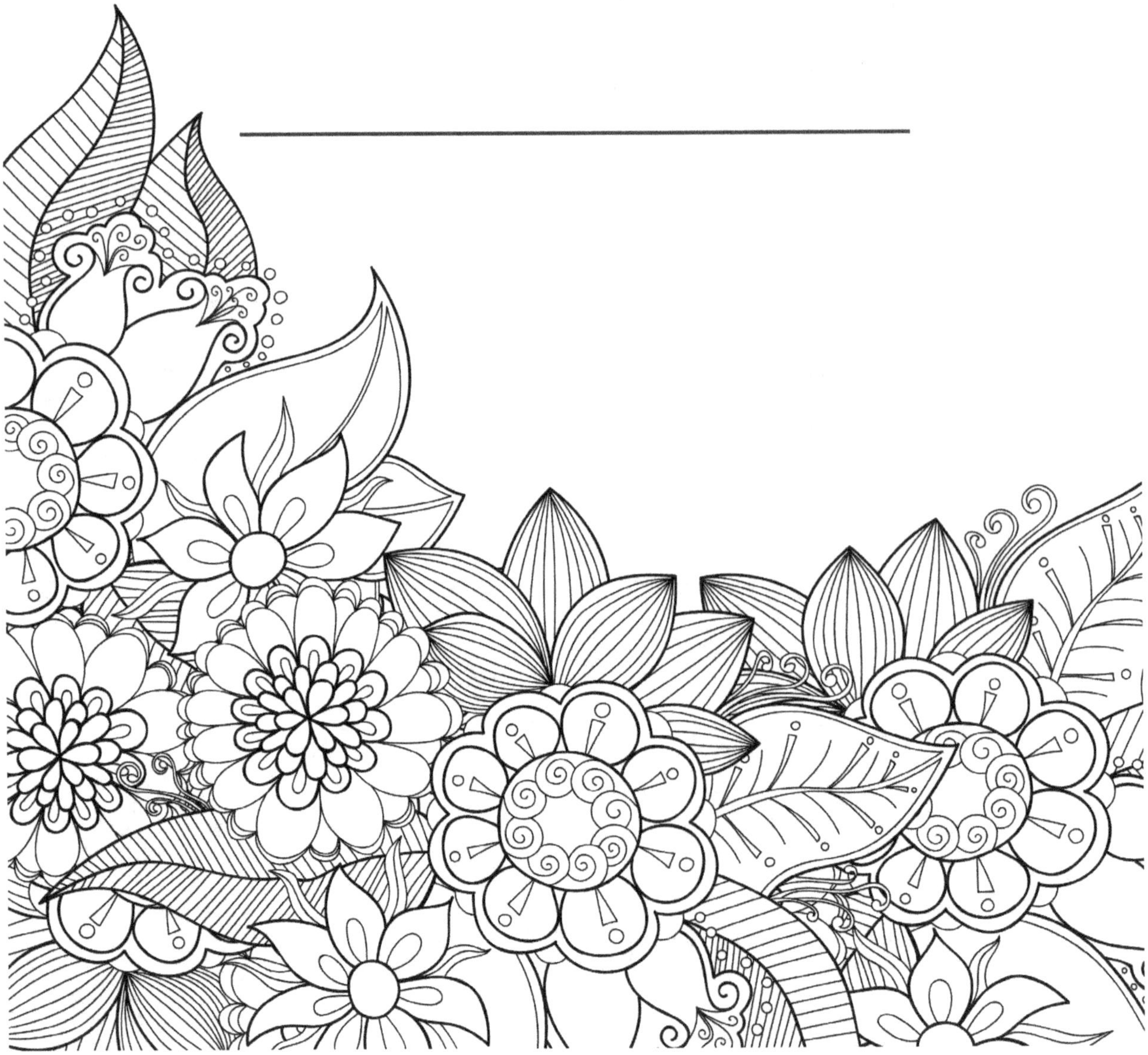

The Lord Reigns
Psalms 97:1

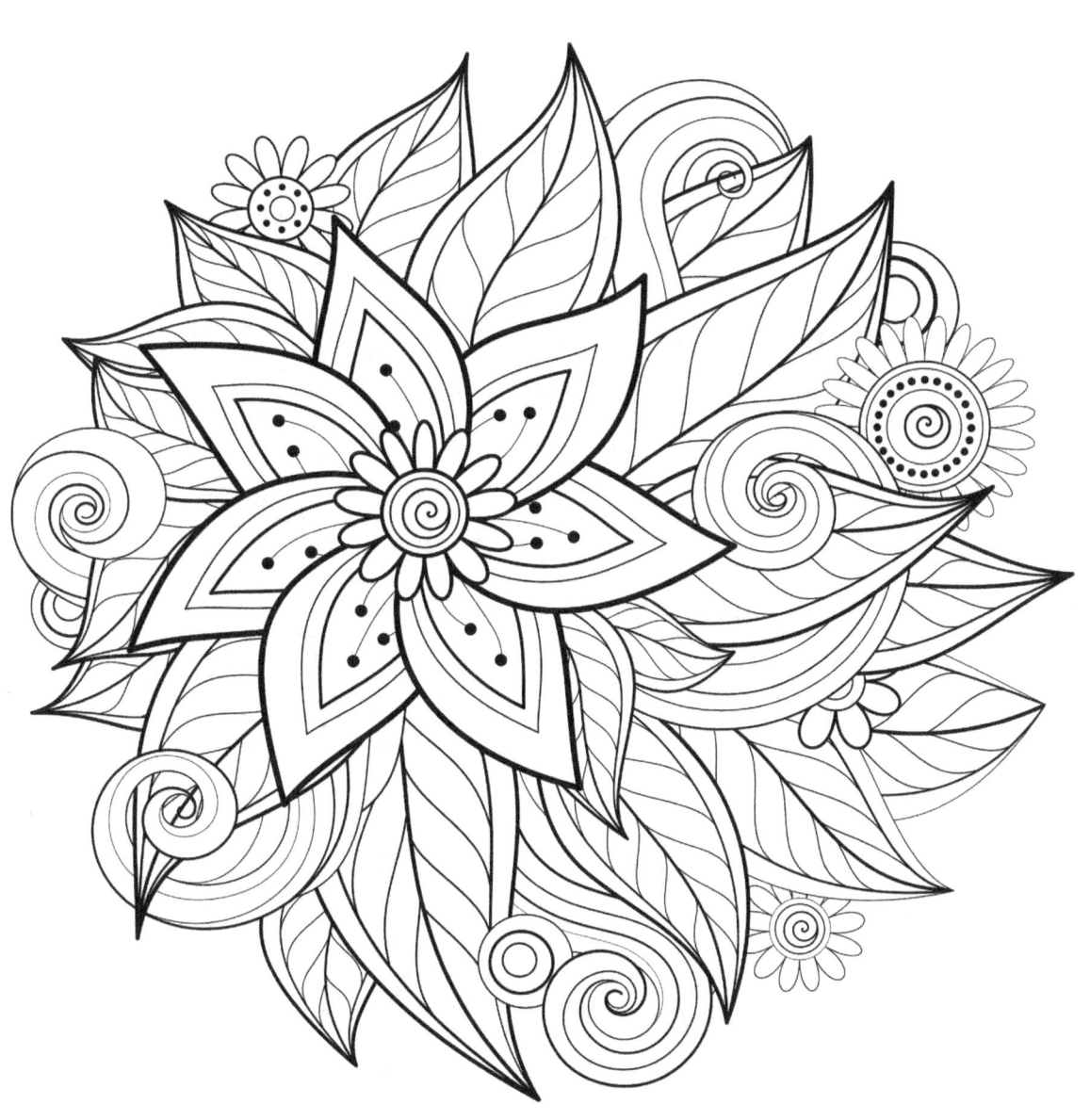

He teaches my hands to war.

Psalms 18:34

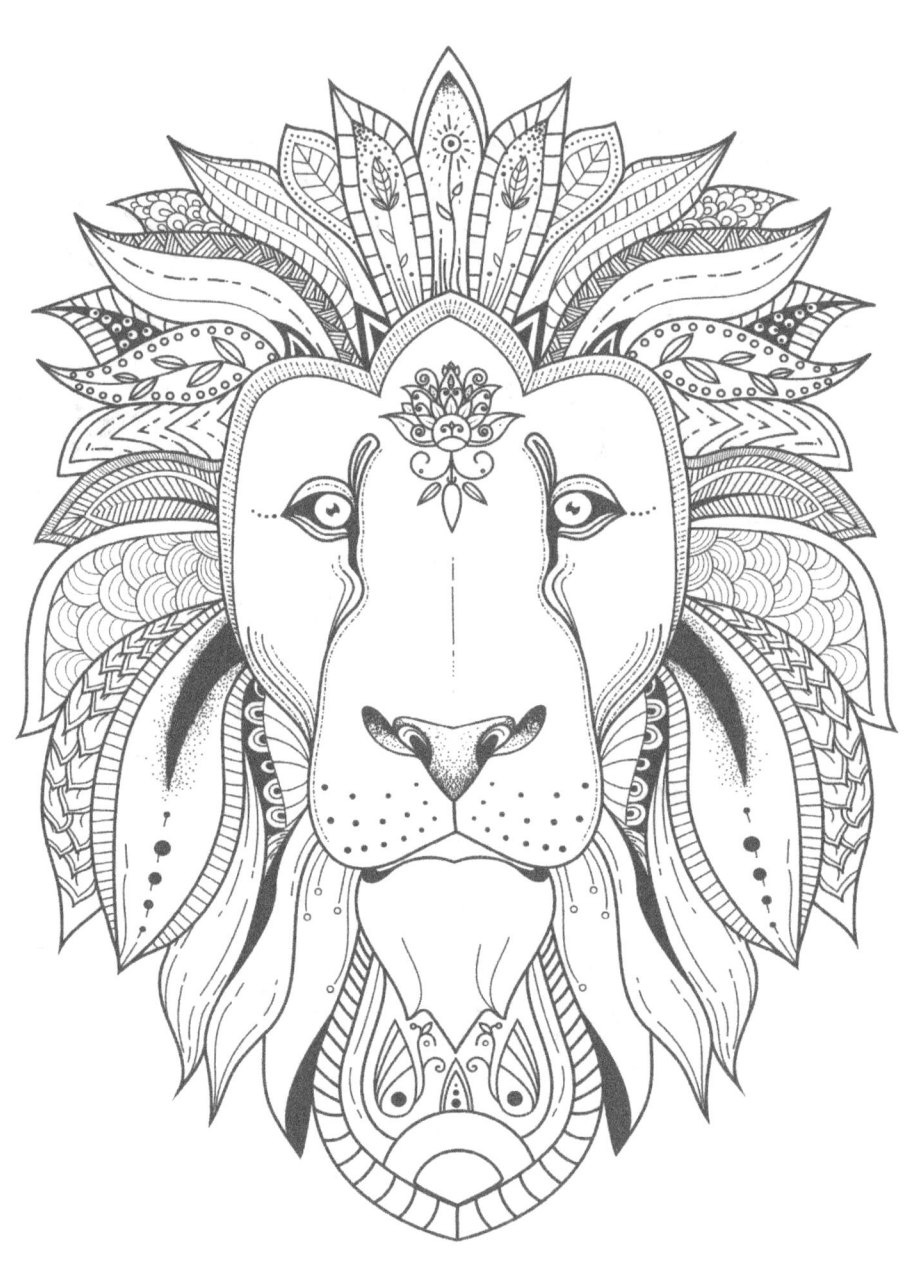

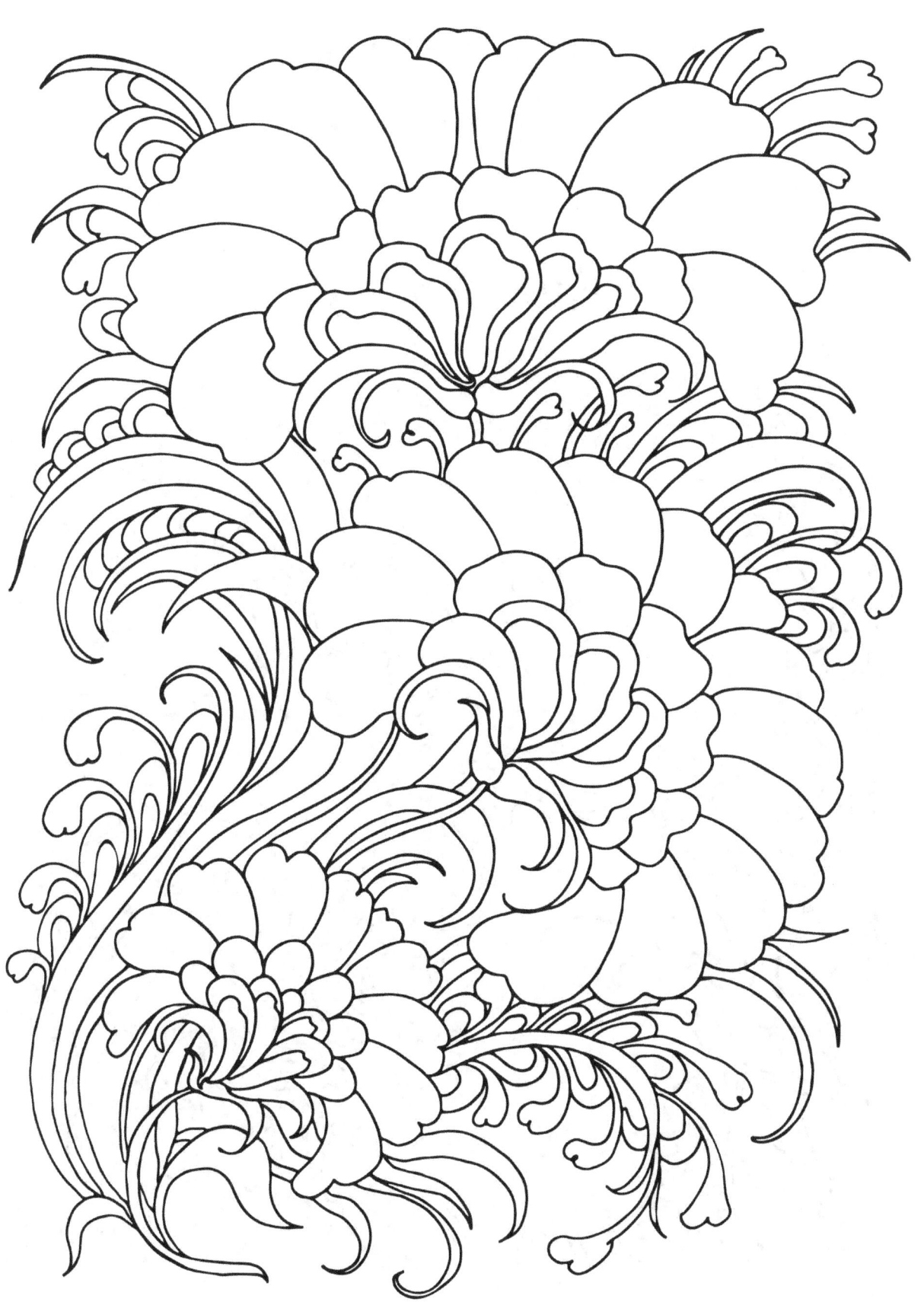

I am more than a conqueror.

Romans 8:37

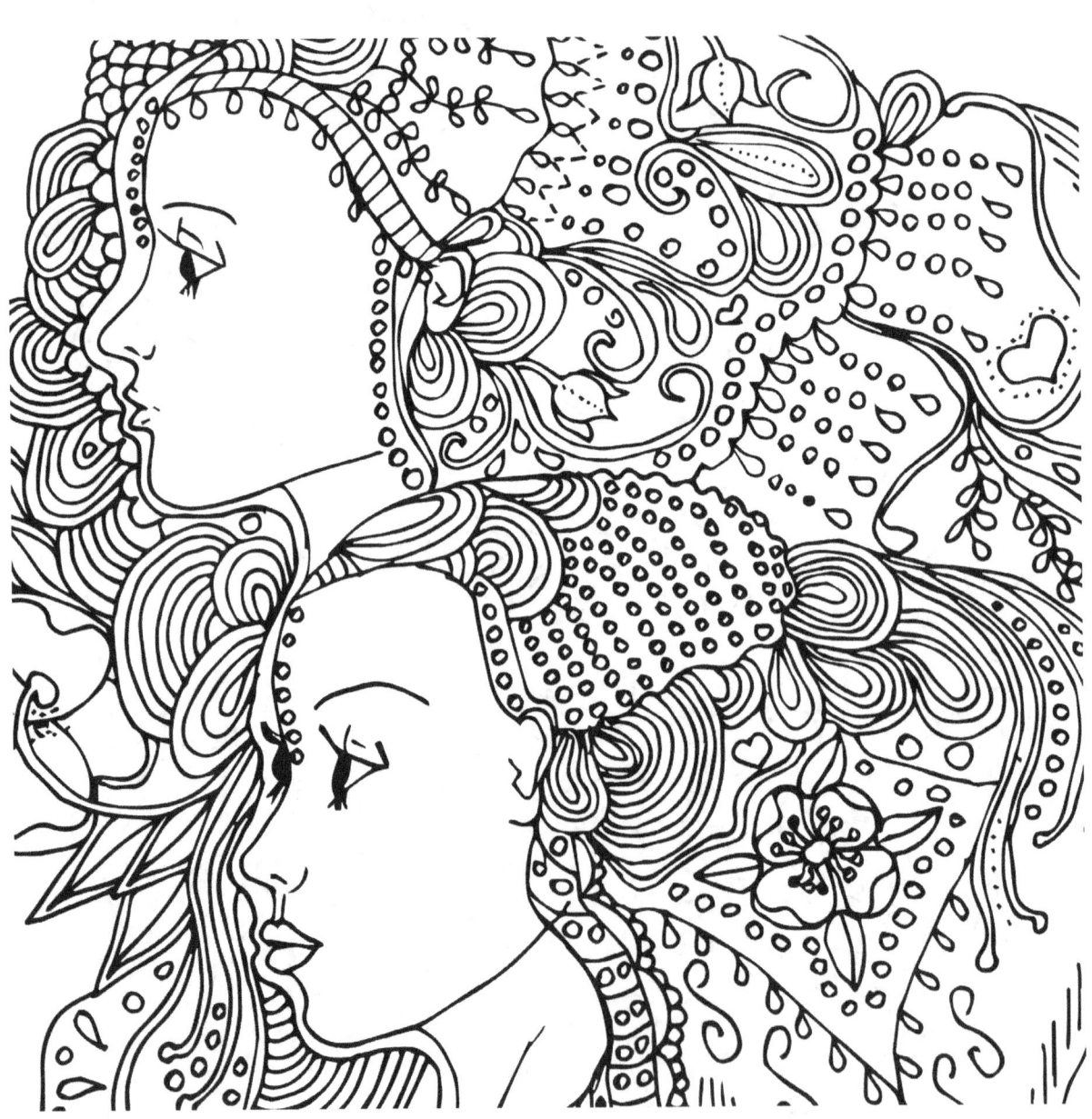

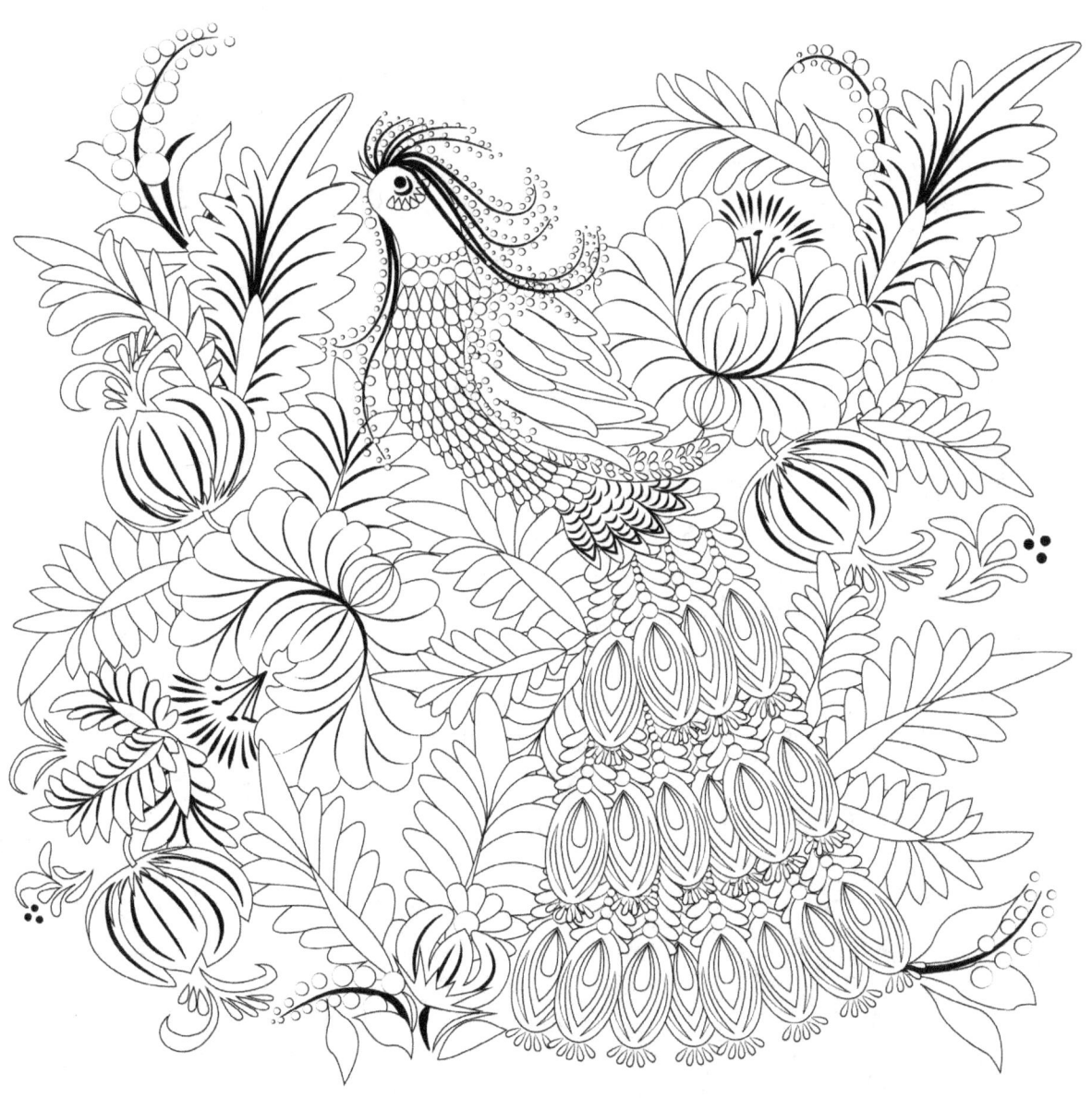

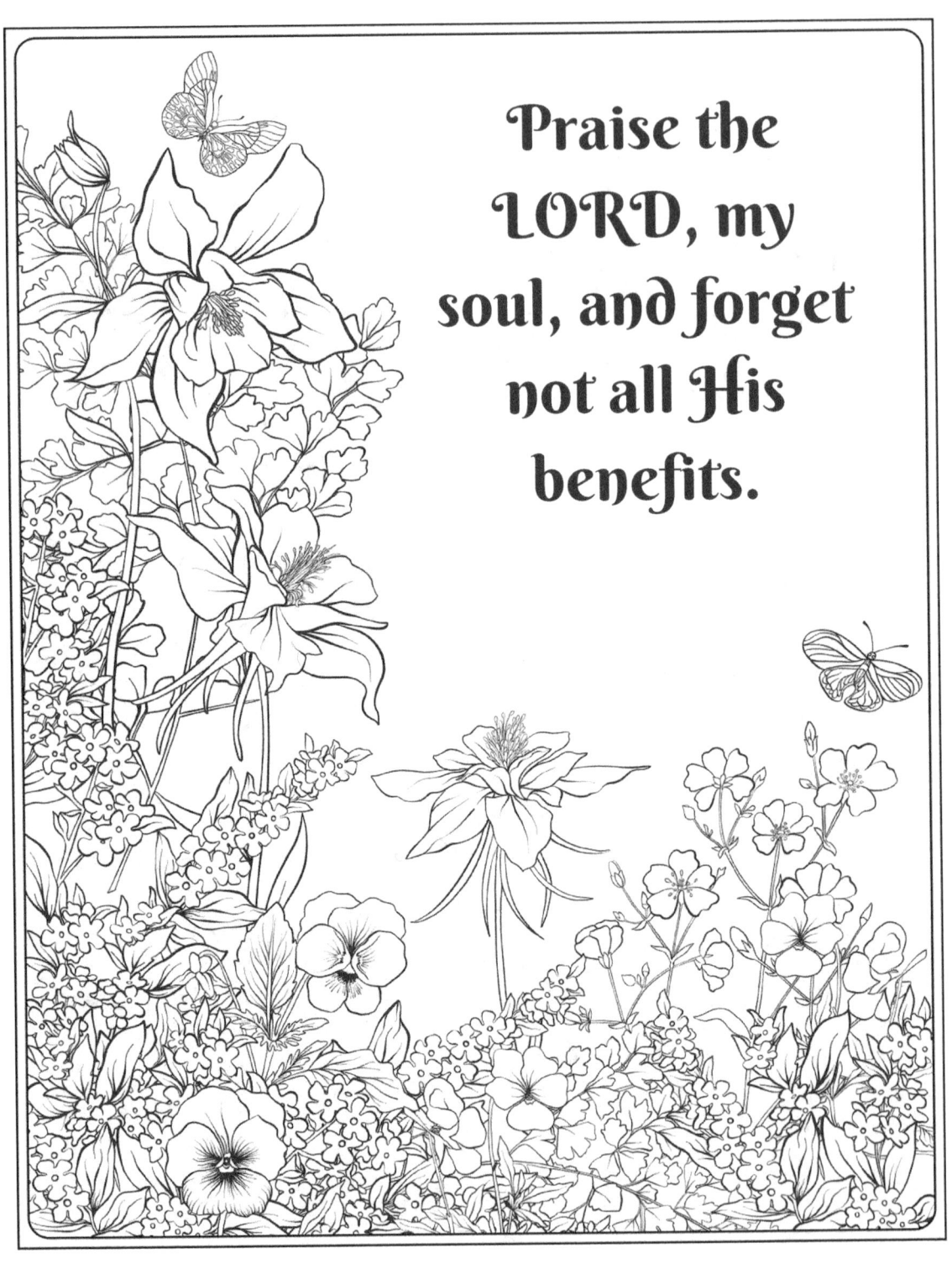

Praise the LORD, my soul, and forget not all His benefits.

Who forgives all your sins
and heals all your
diseases, who redeems
your life from the
pit and crowns you with
love and compassion,
who satisfies your desires
with good things so that
your youth is renewed like
the eagle's.

Psalms 103:2-5

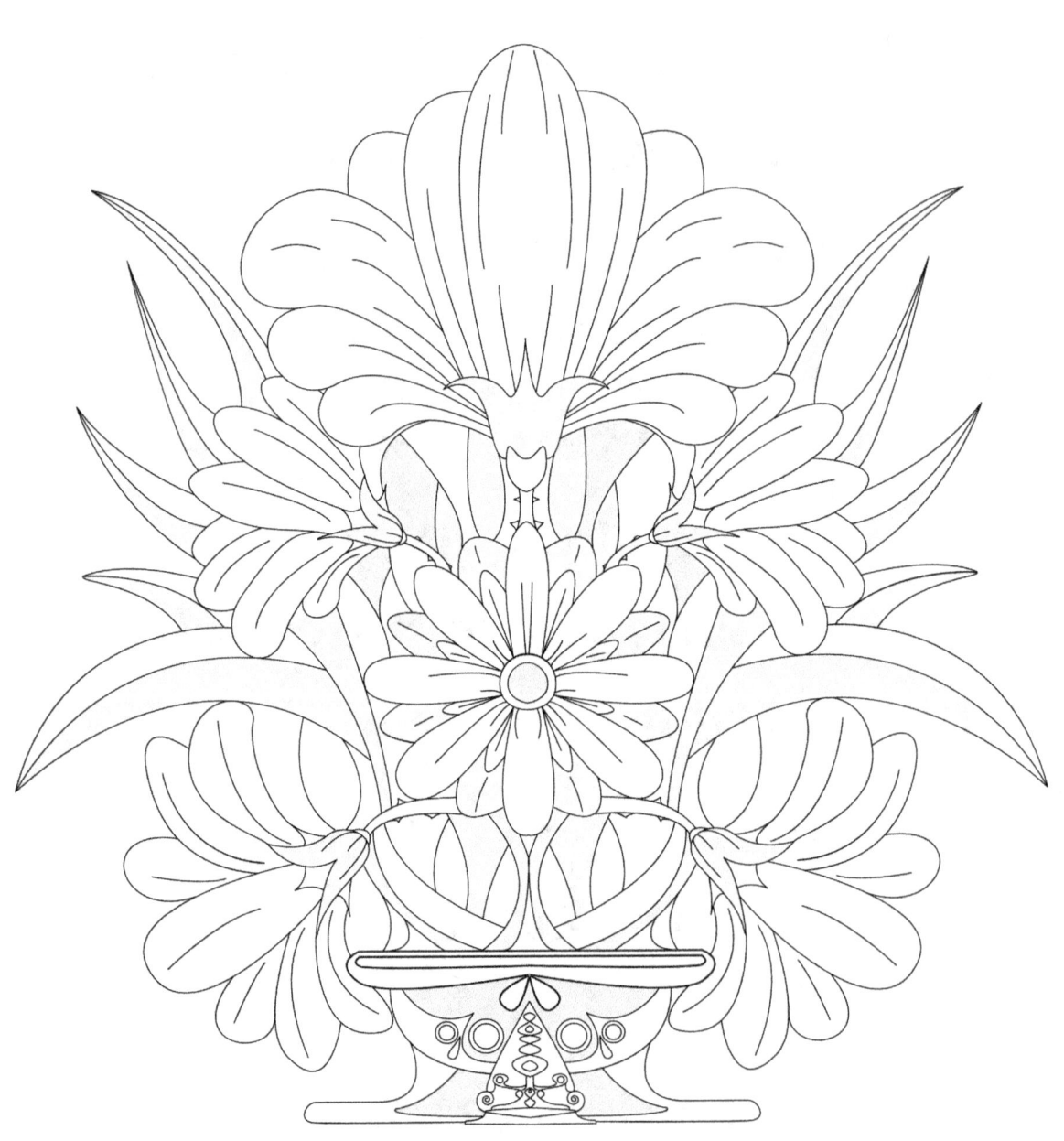

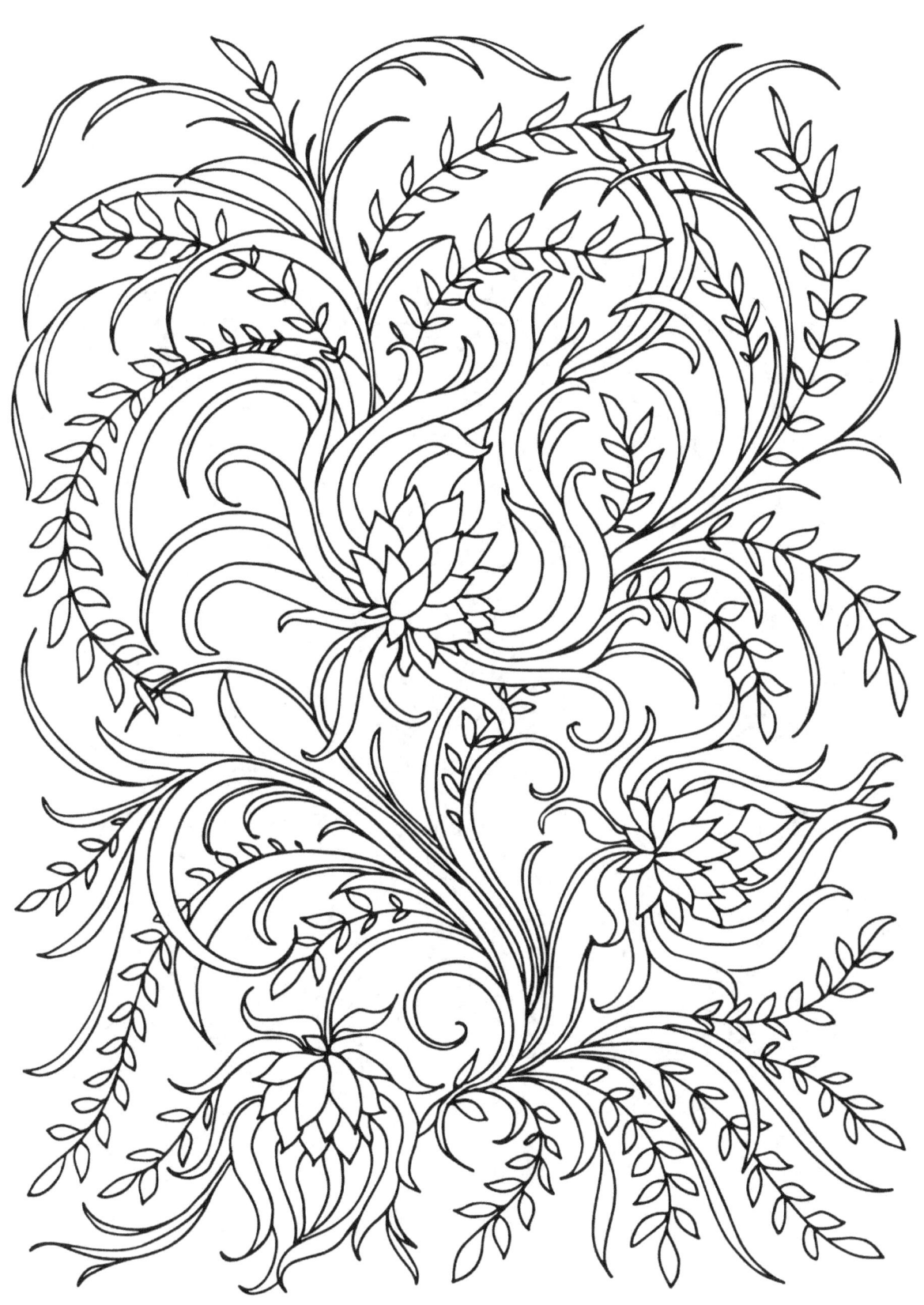

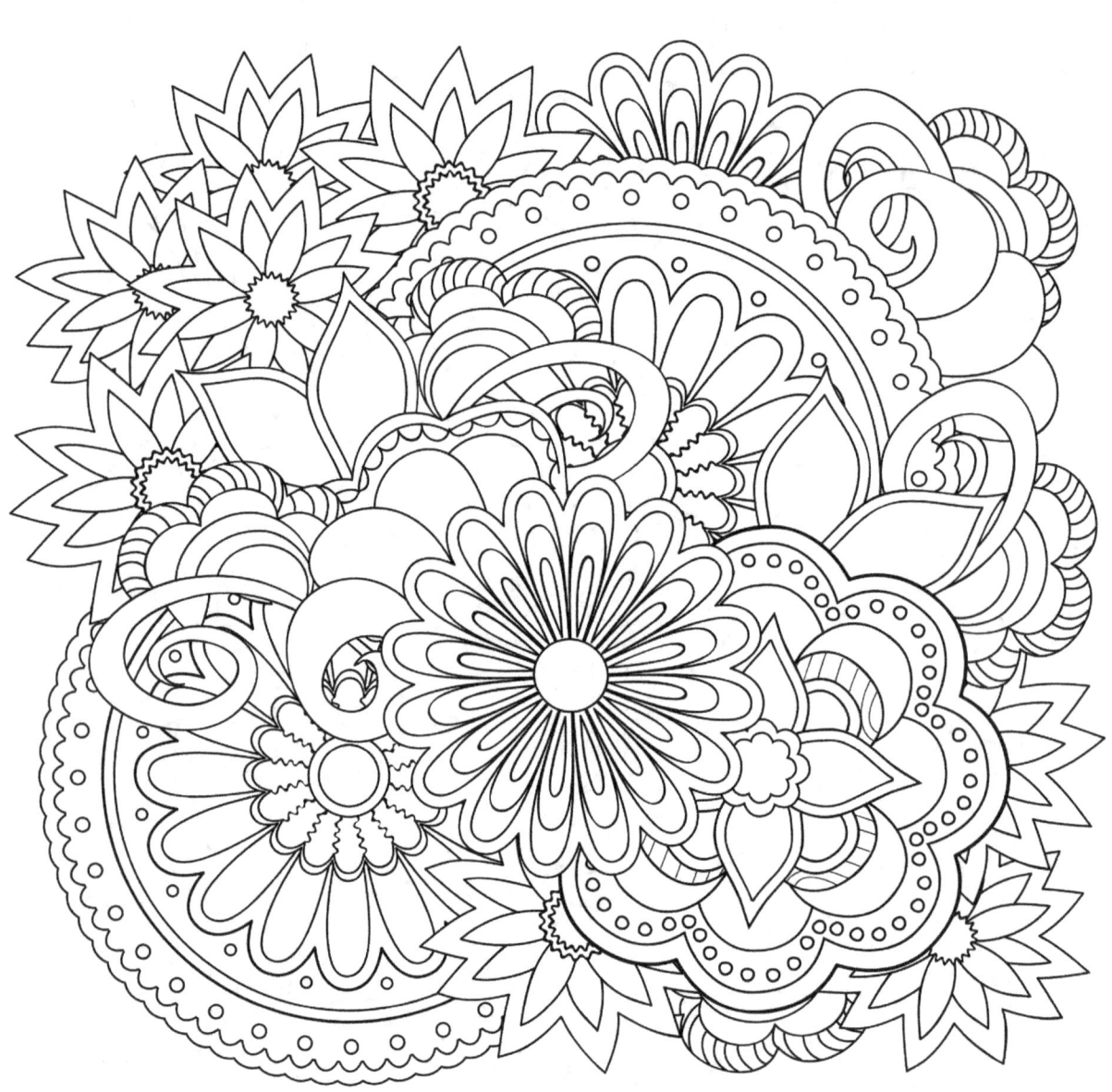

You will keep him in
perfect peace,
whose mind is stayed
on You,
Because he trusts in
You.

Isaiah 26: 3

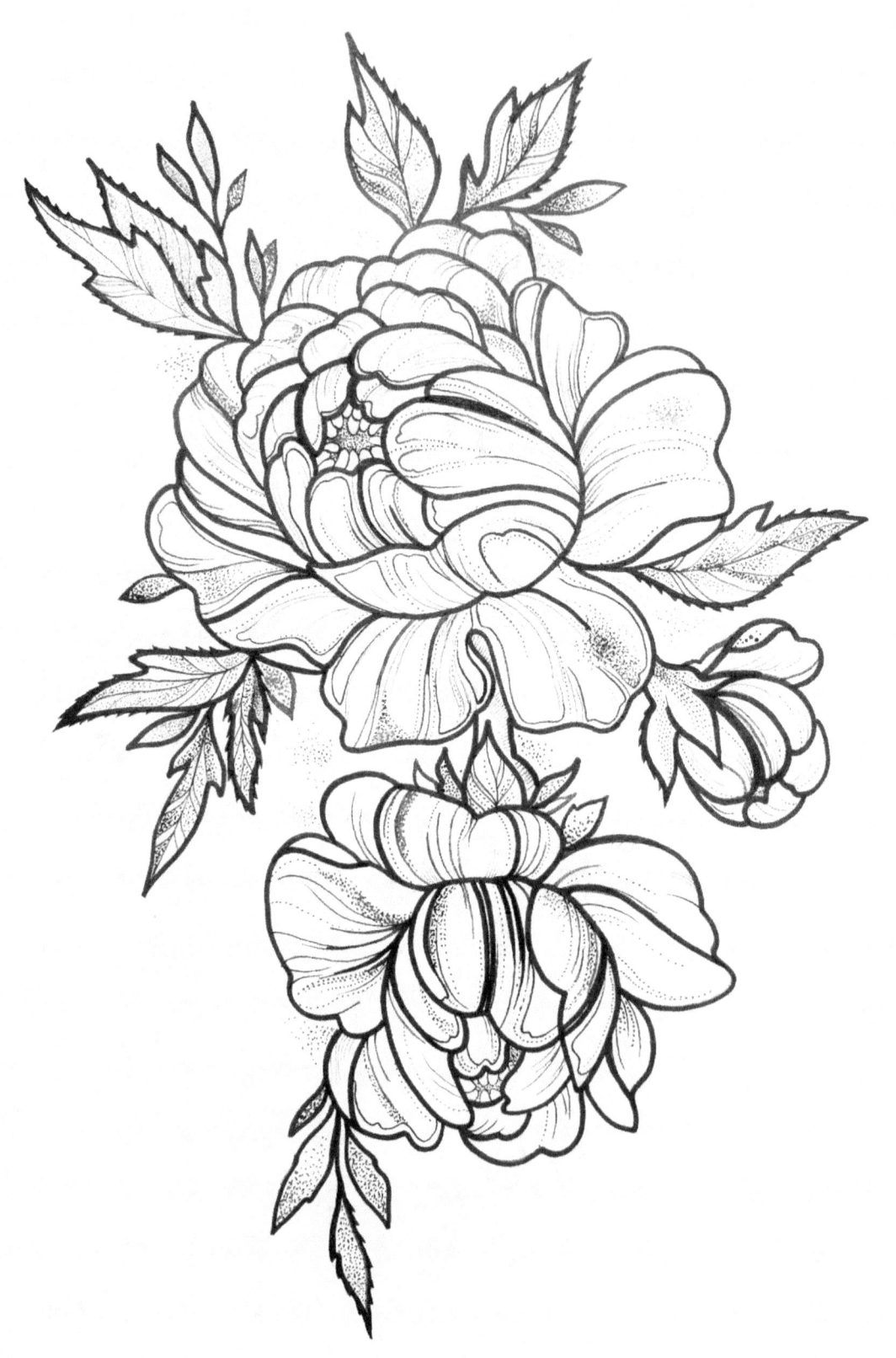

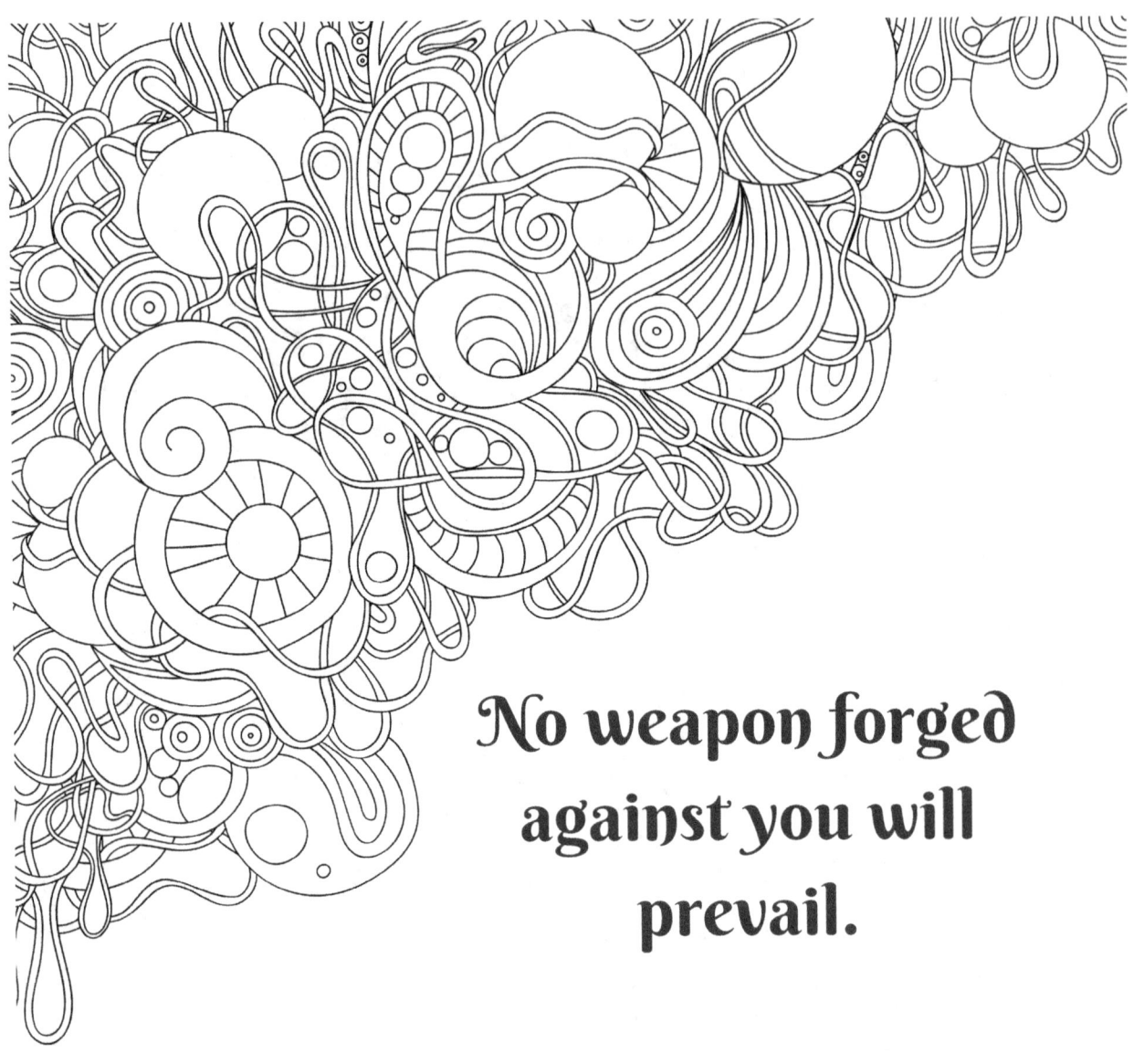

No weapon forged against you will prevail.

Isaiah 54:17

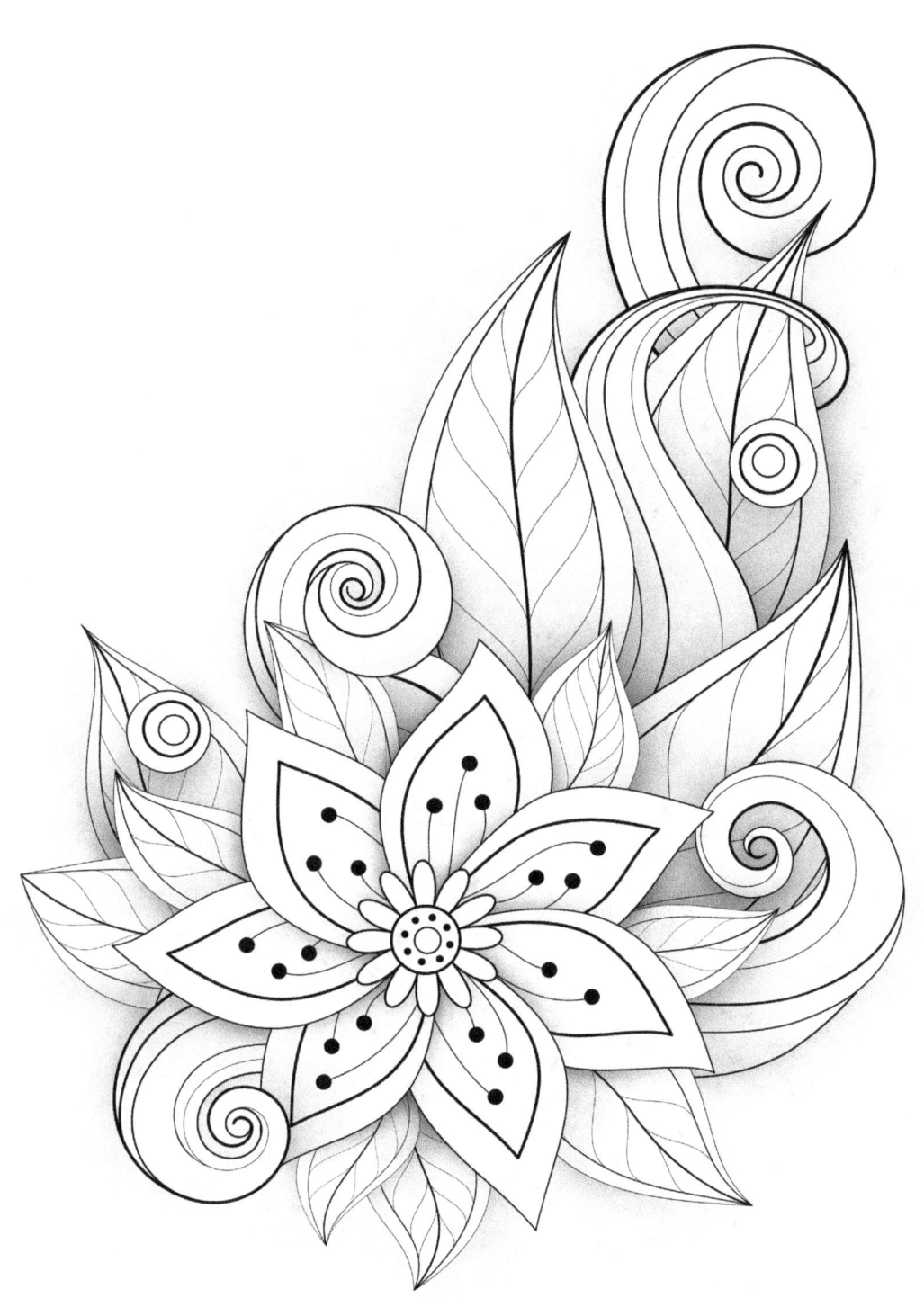

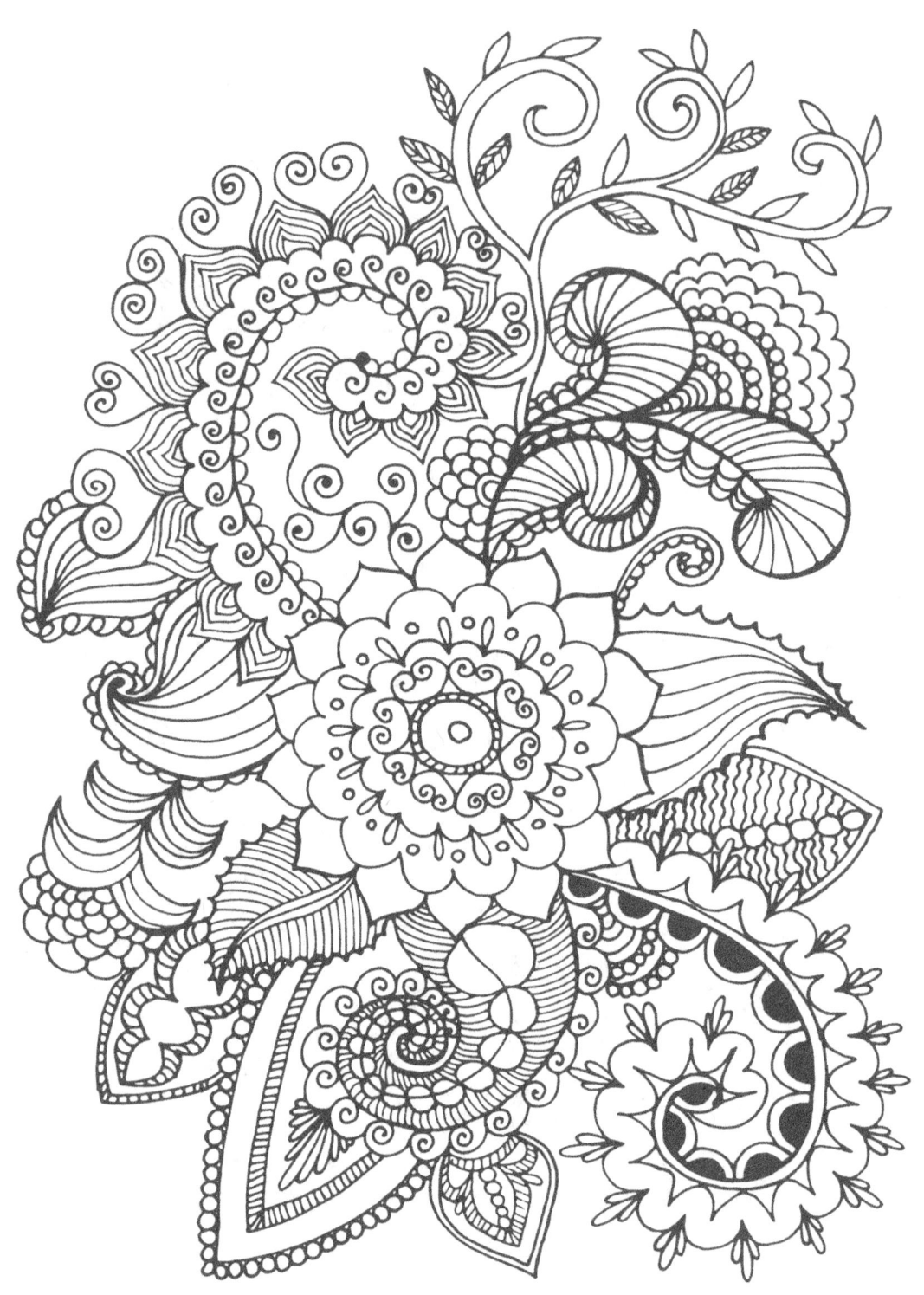

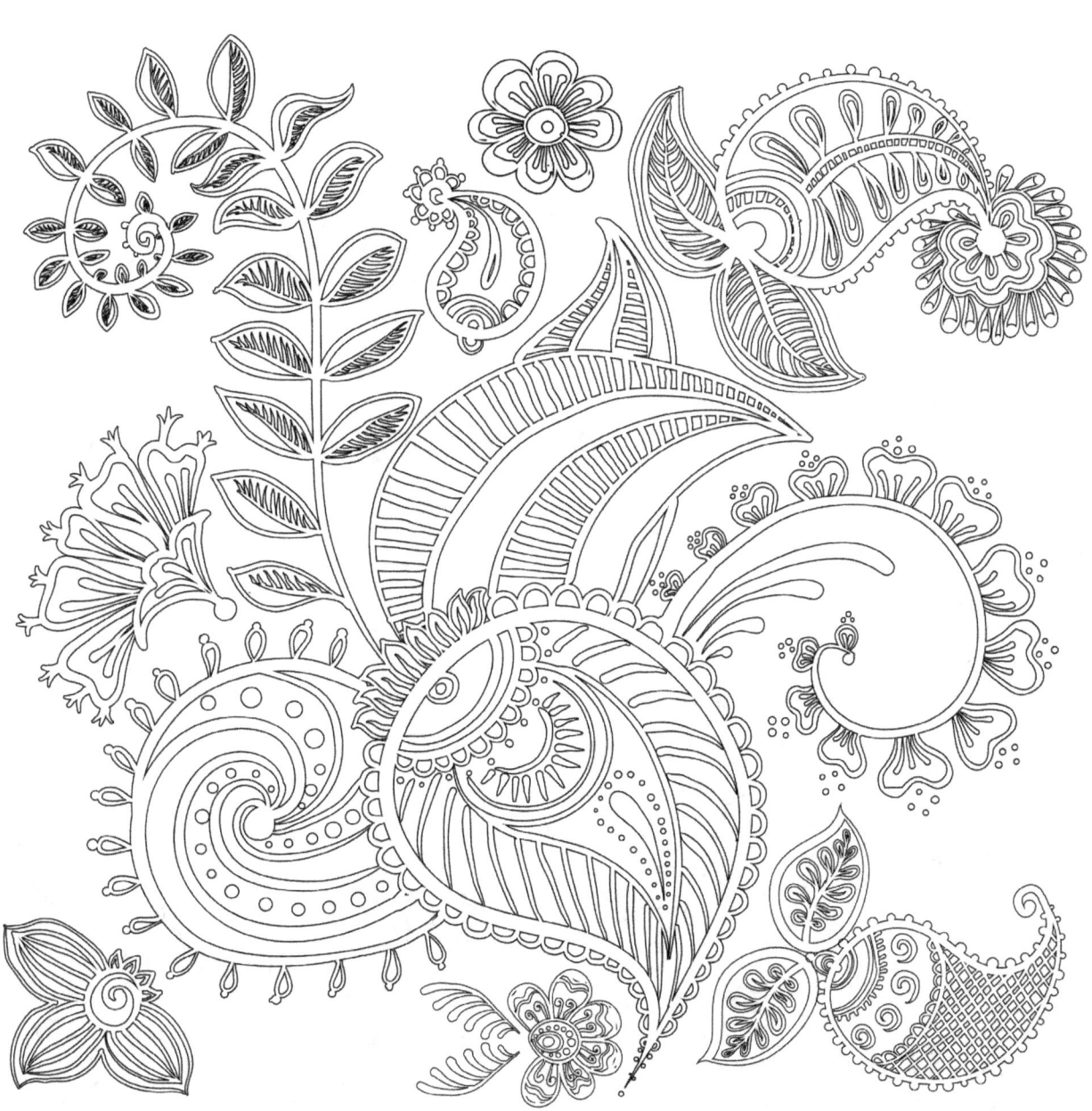

For I am the LORD your
God who takes hold of your
right hand and says to you,
Do not fear;
I will help you.

Isaiah 41:13

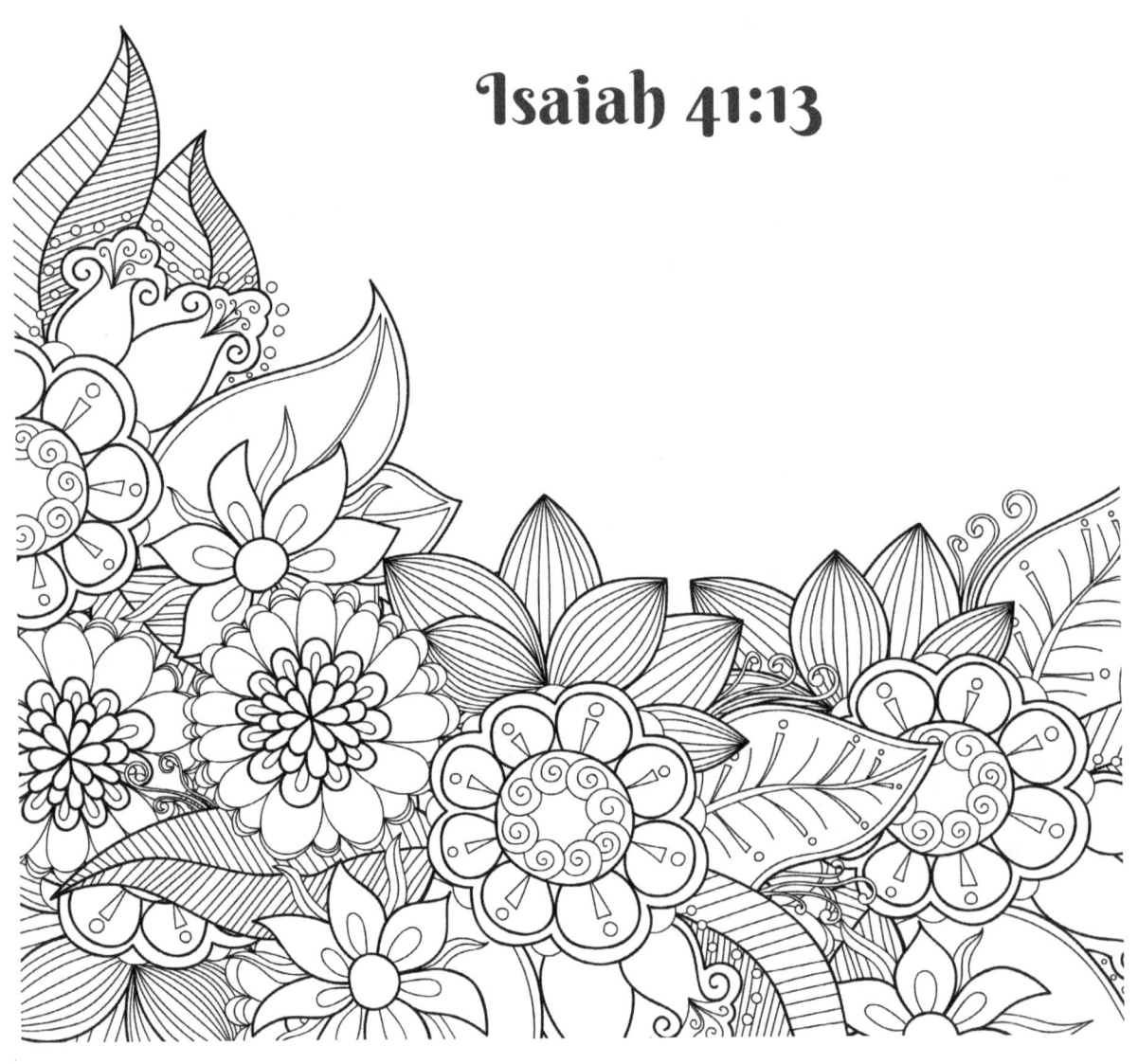

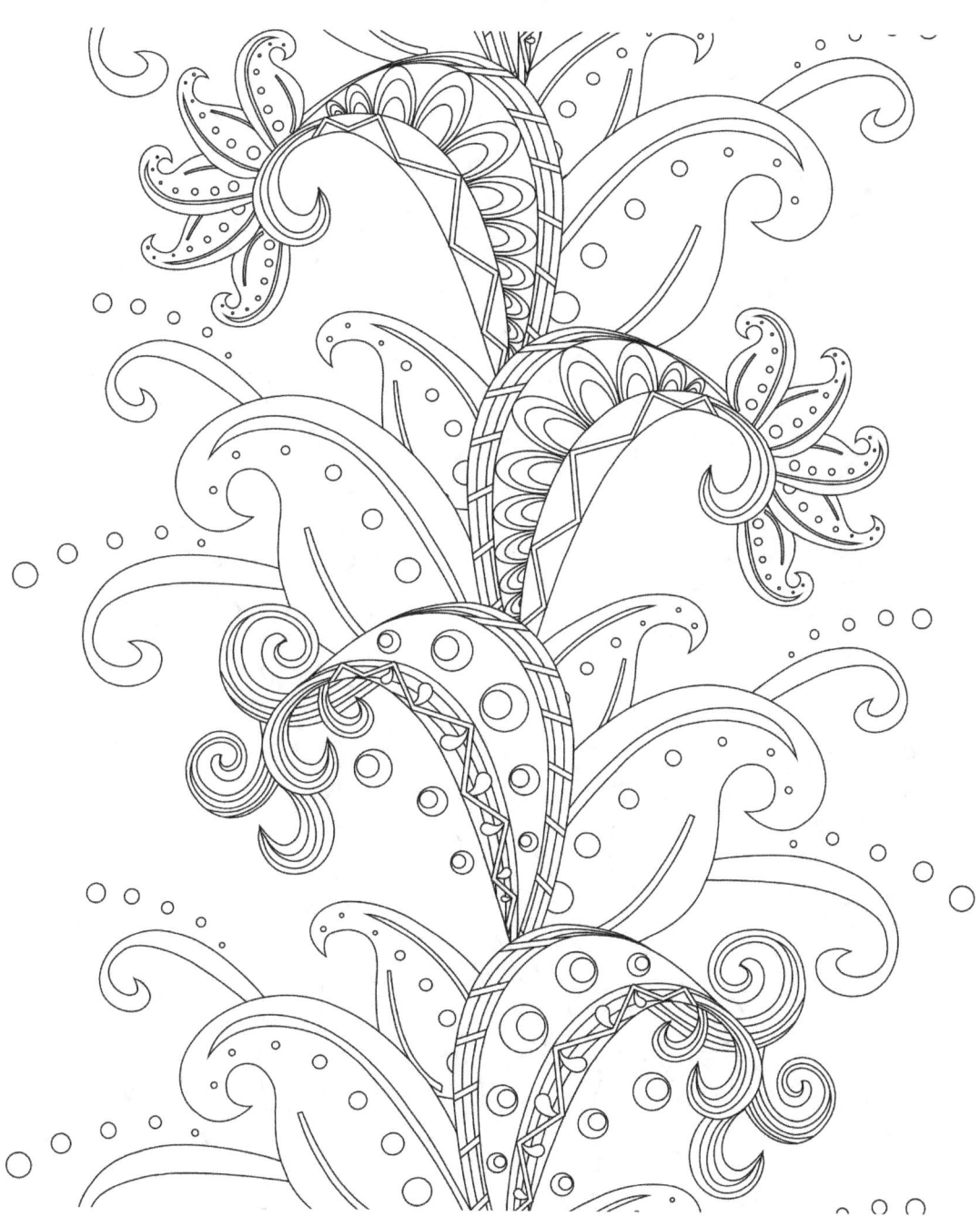

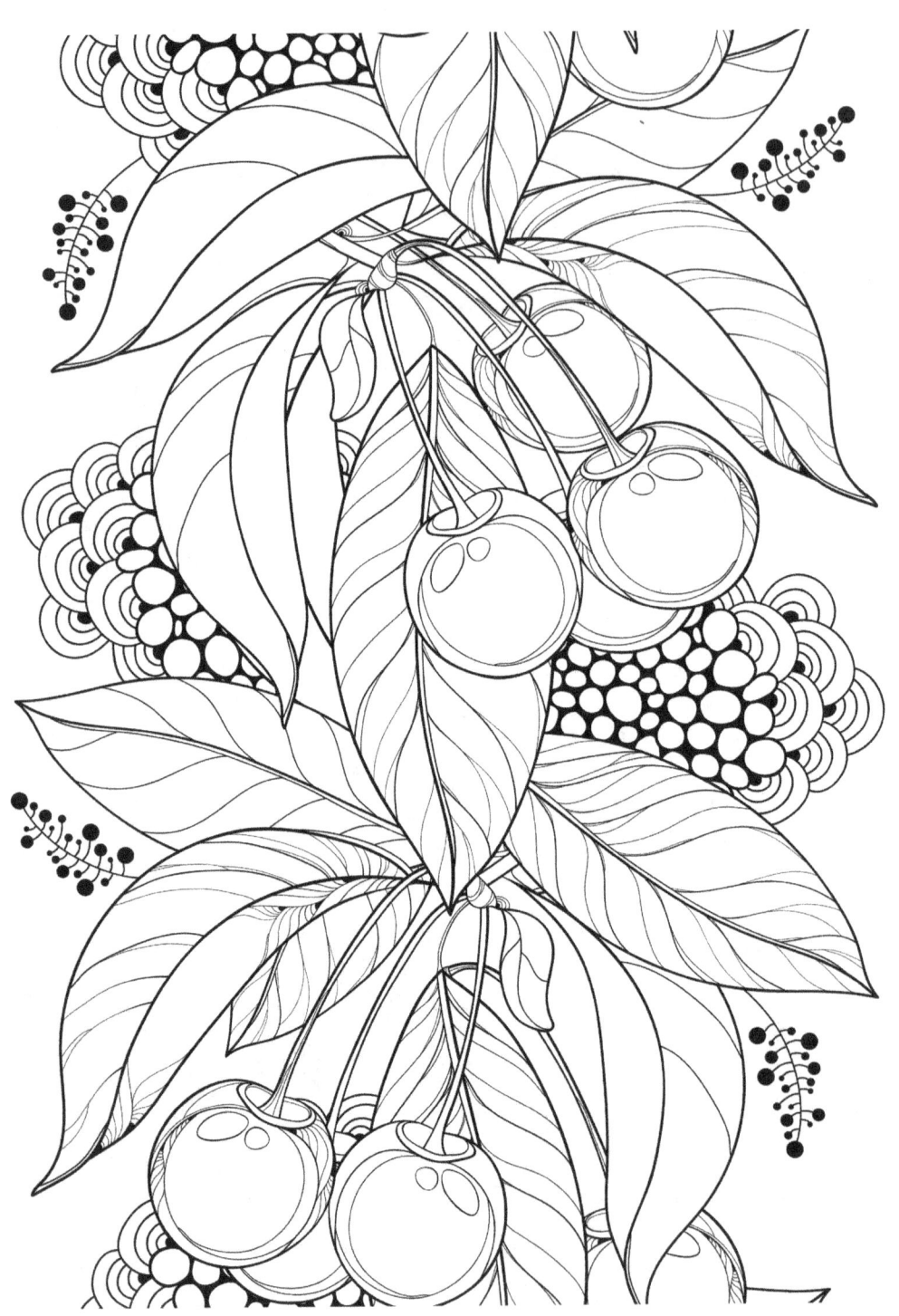

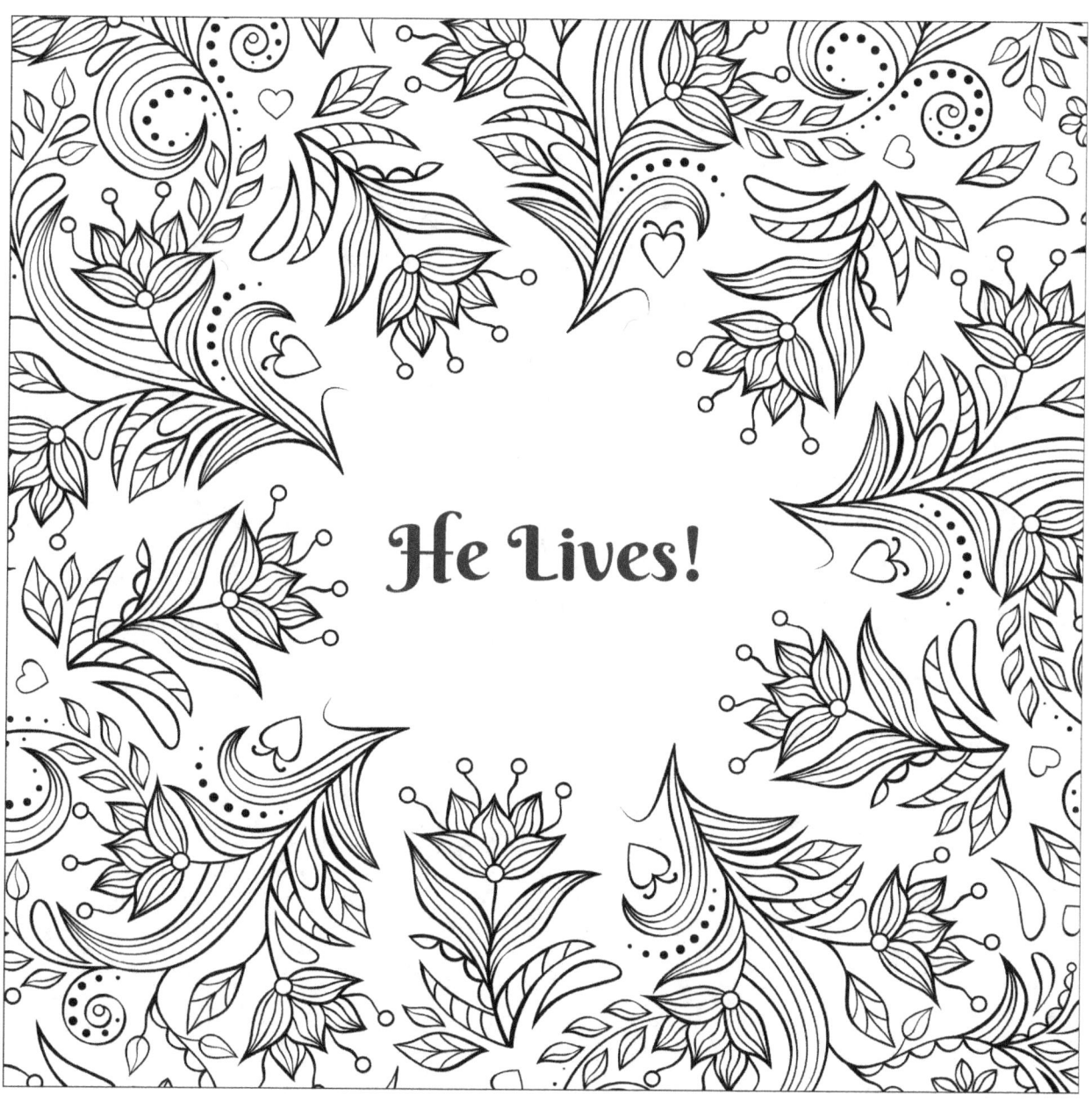

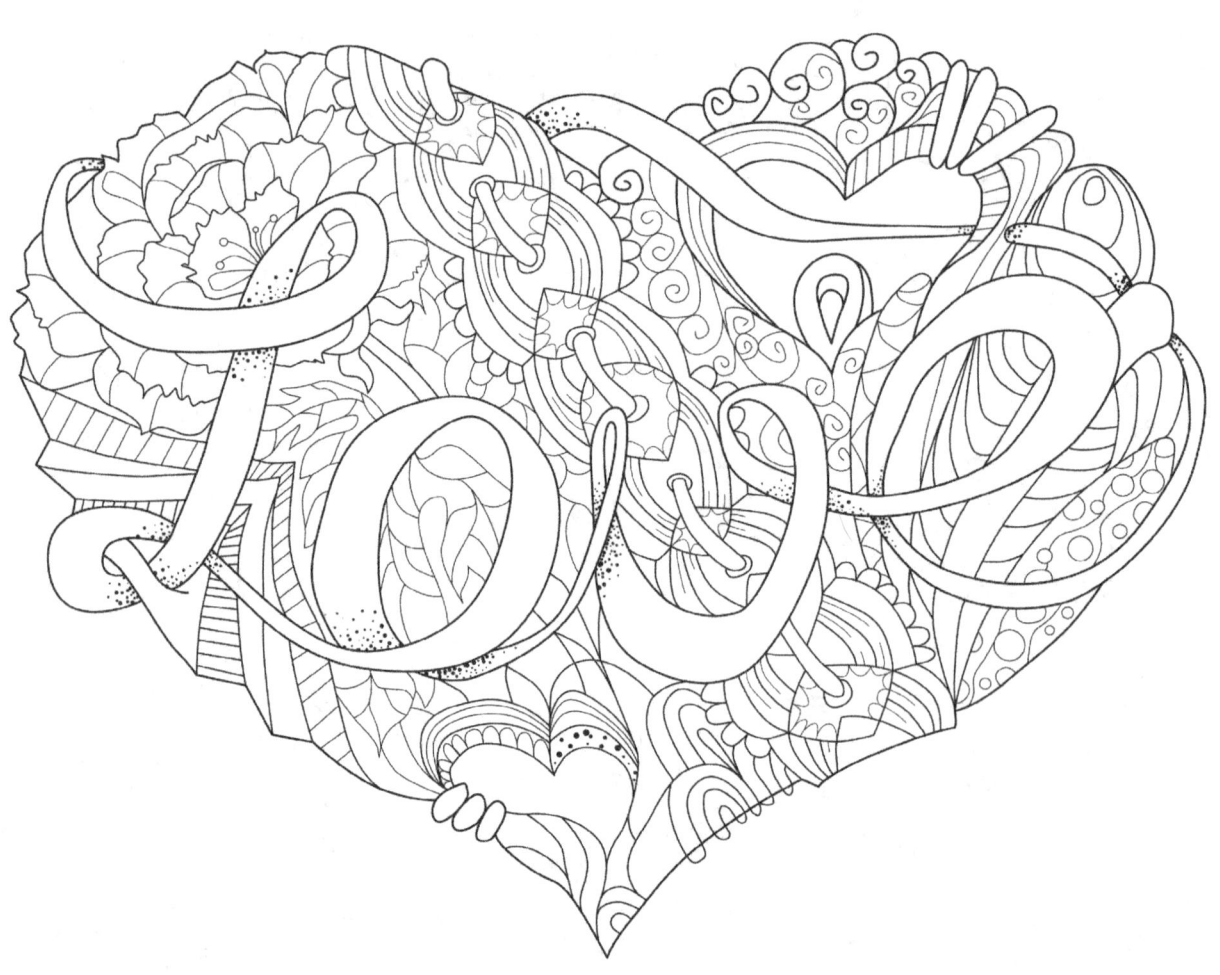

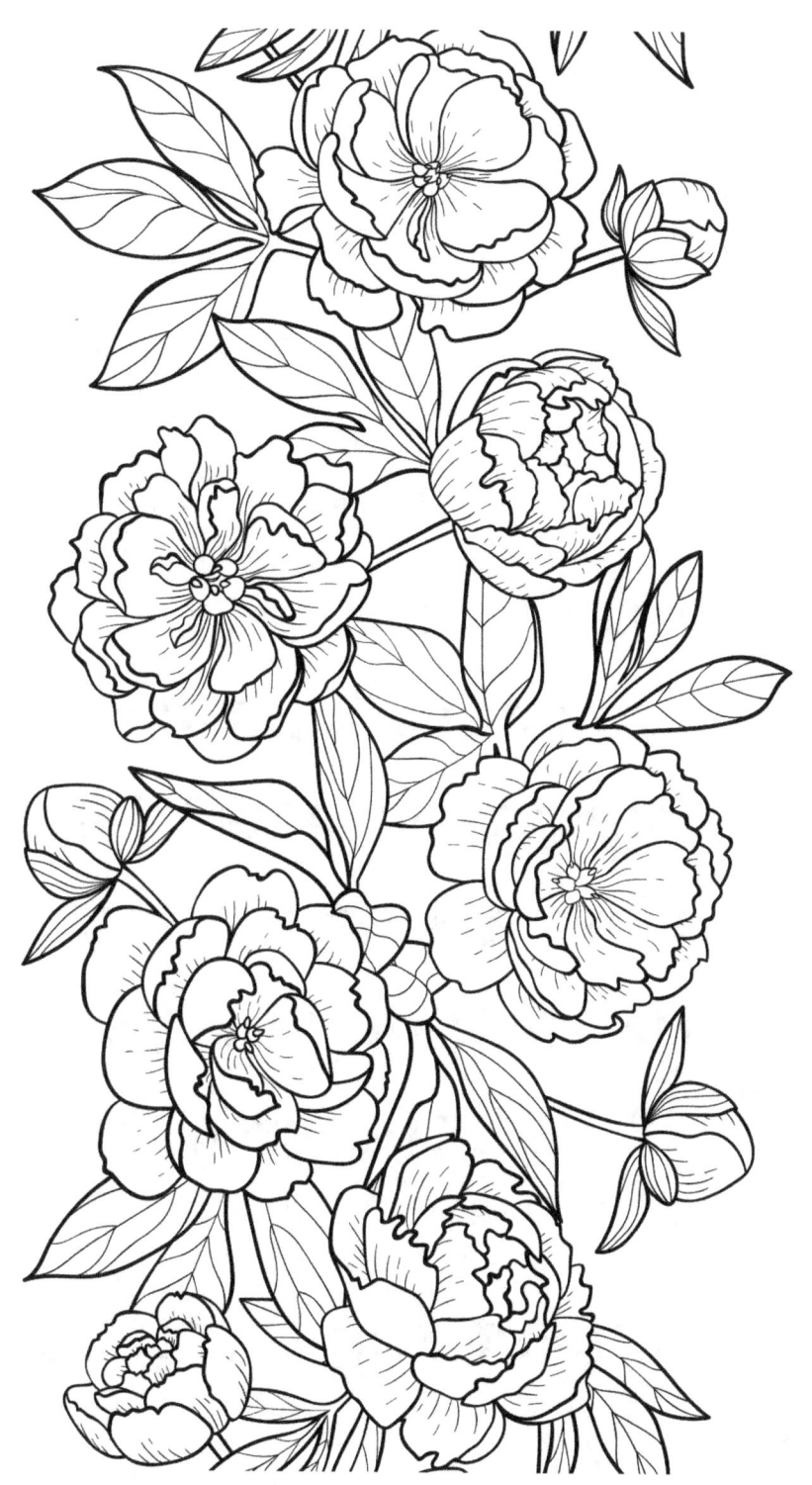

Because of the LORD's great love we are not consumed, for his compassions never fail. They are new every morning; great is your faithfulness.

Lamentations 3:22-23

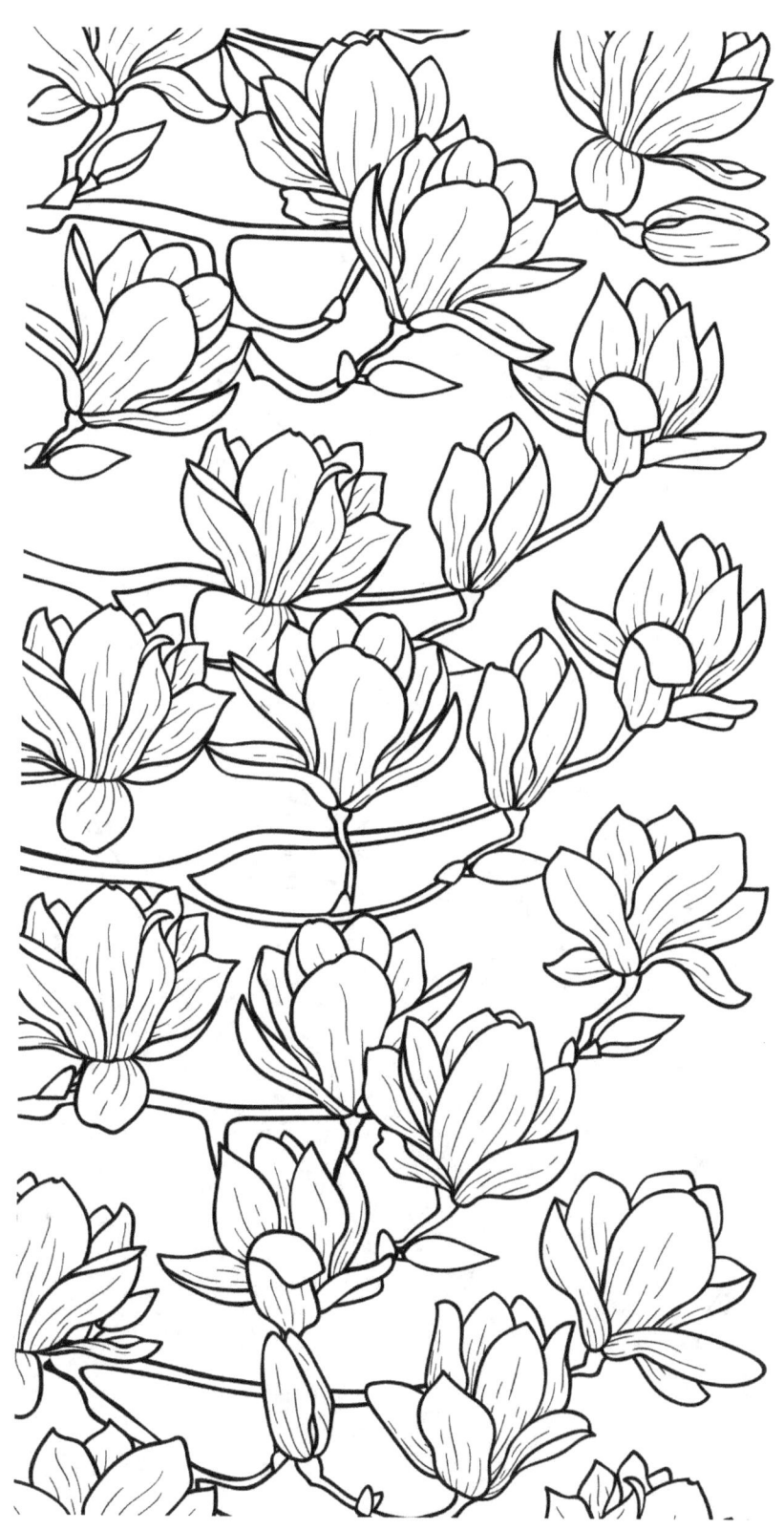

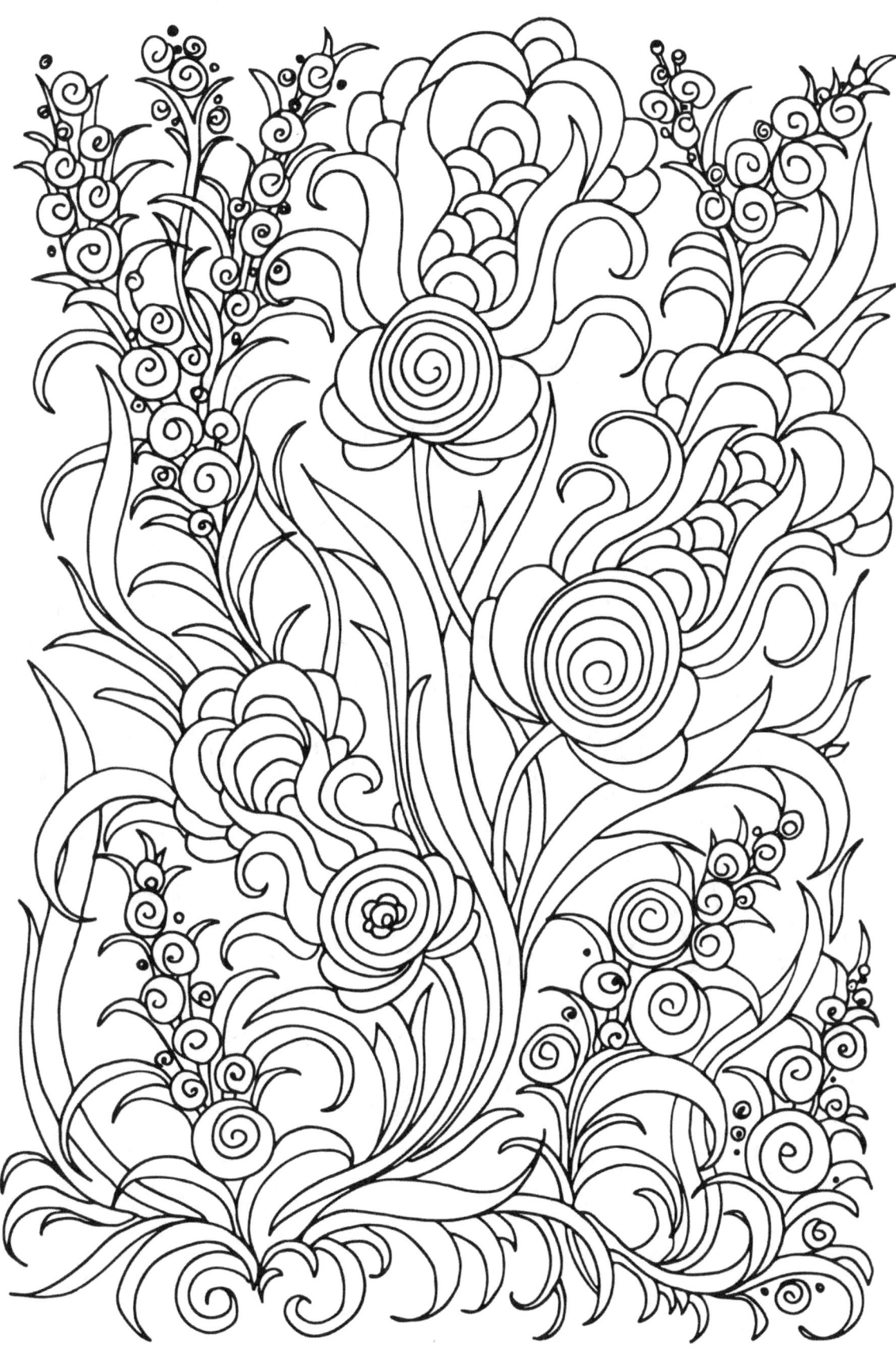

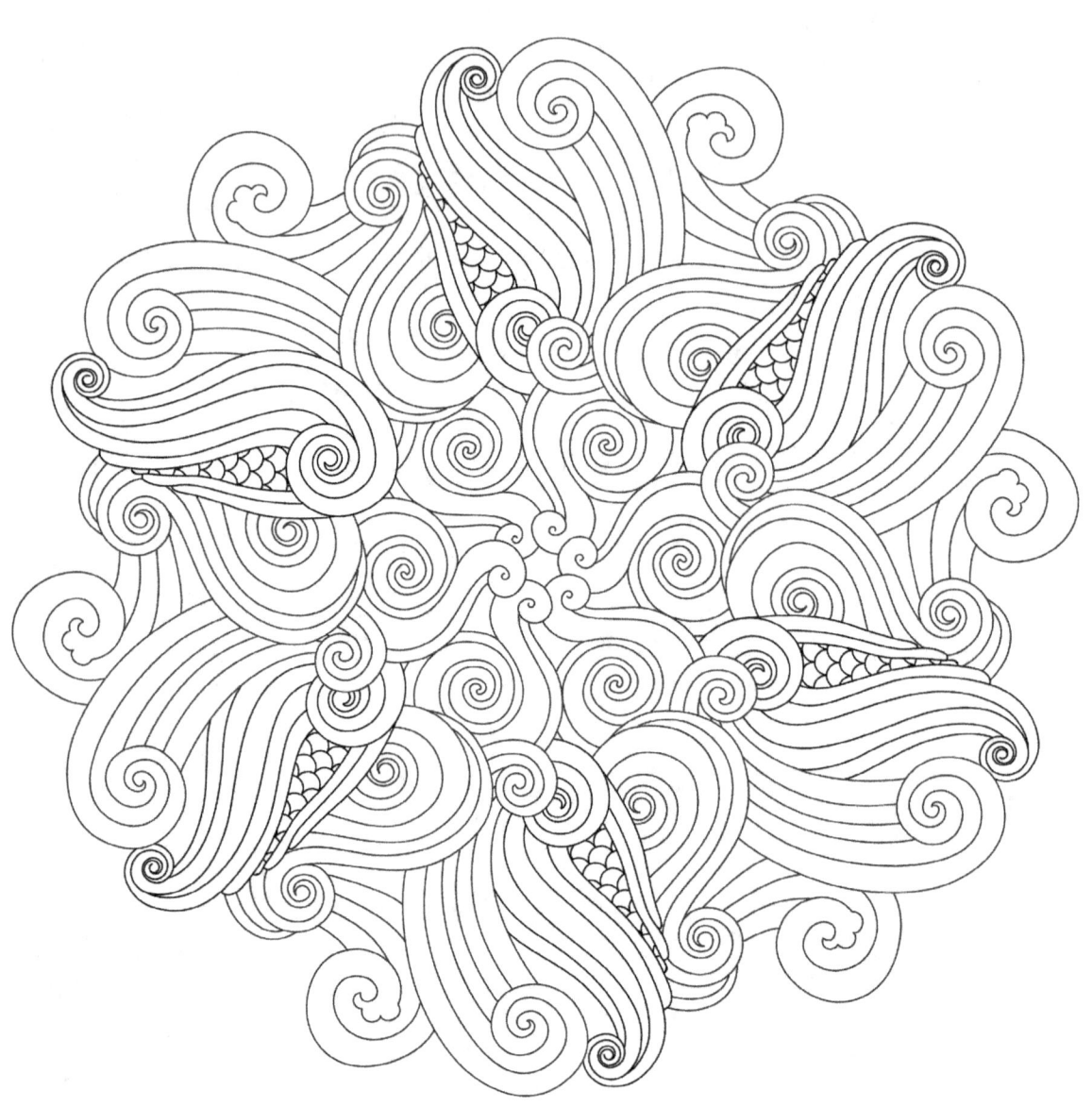

He gives strength to the weary and increases the power of the weak.

Isaiah 40:29

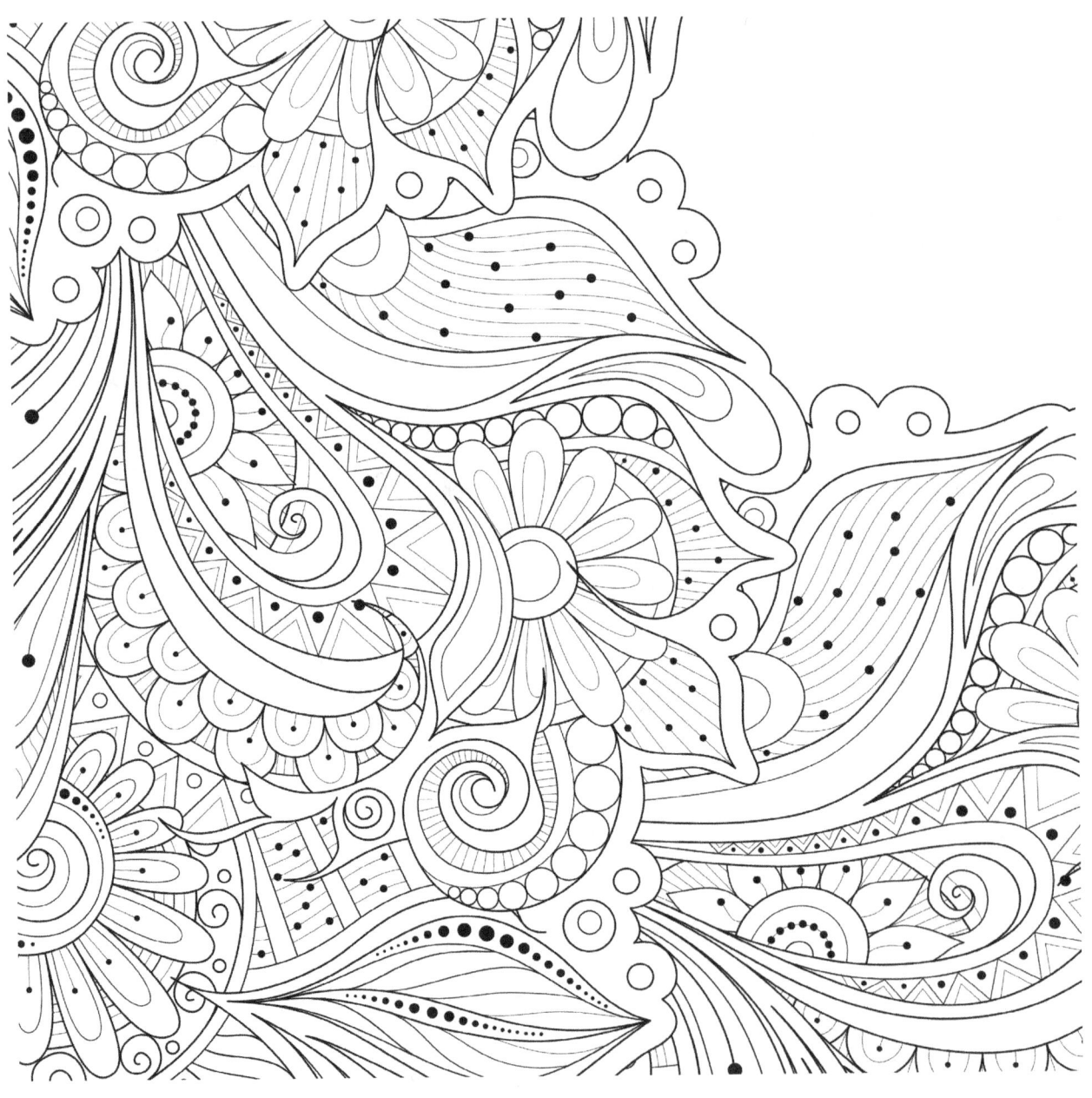

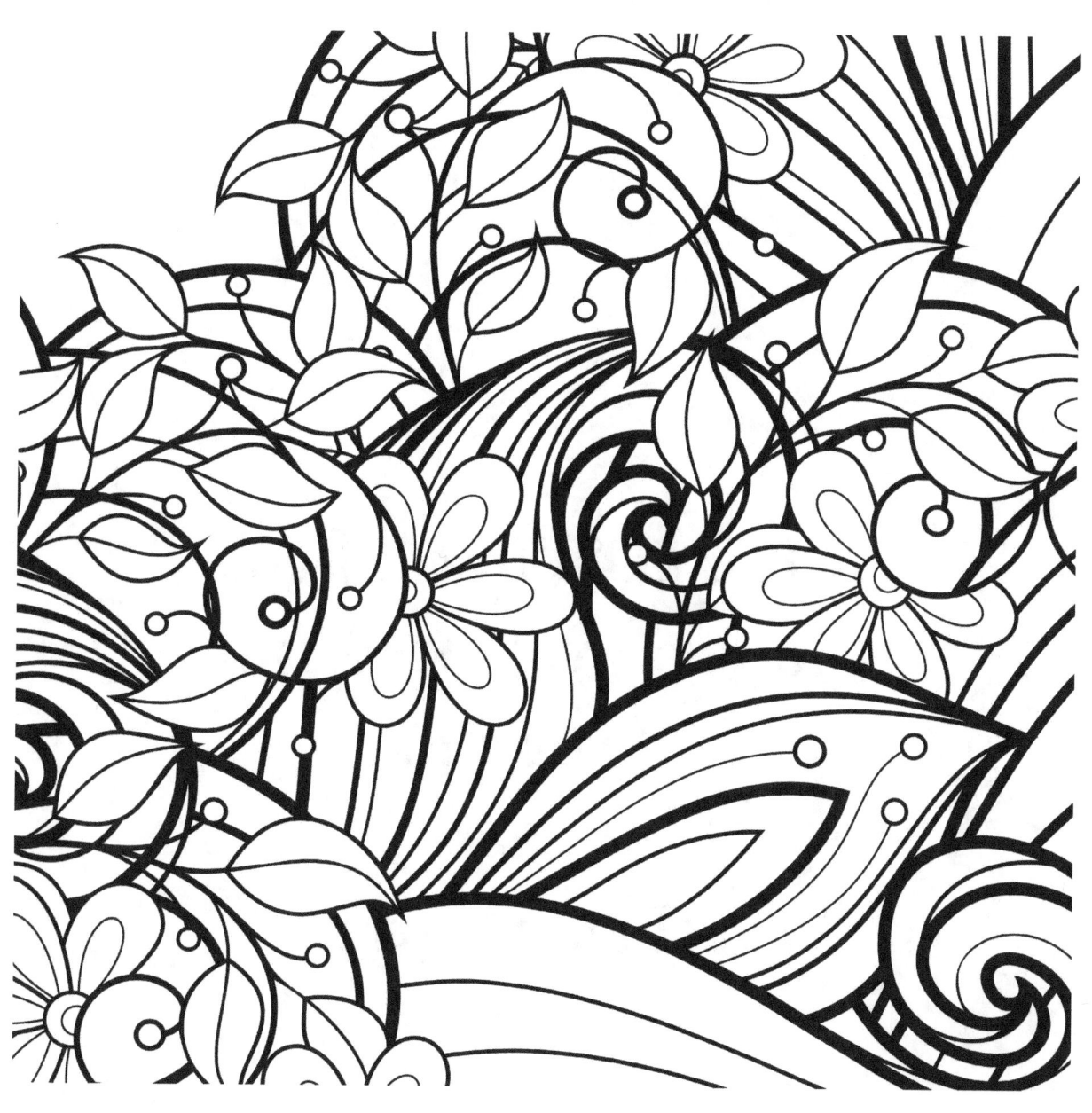

The LORD will fight for you; you need only to be still.

Exodus 14:14

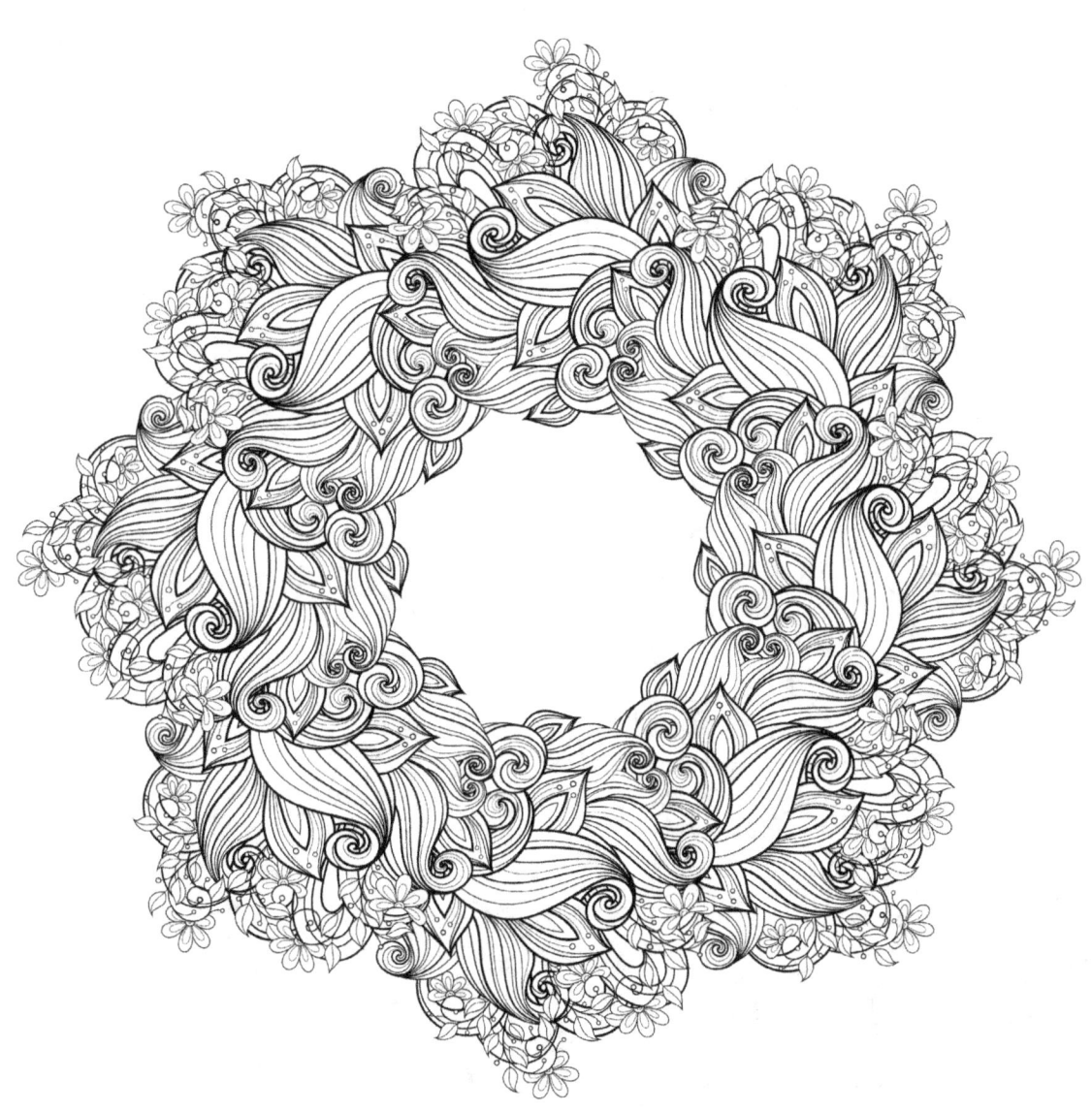

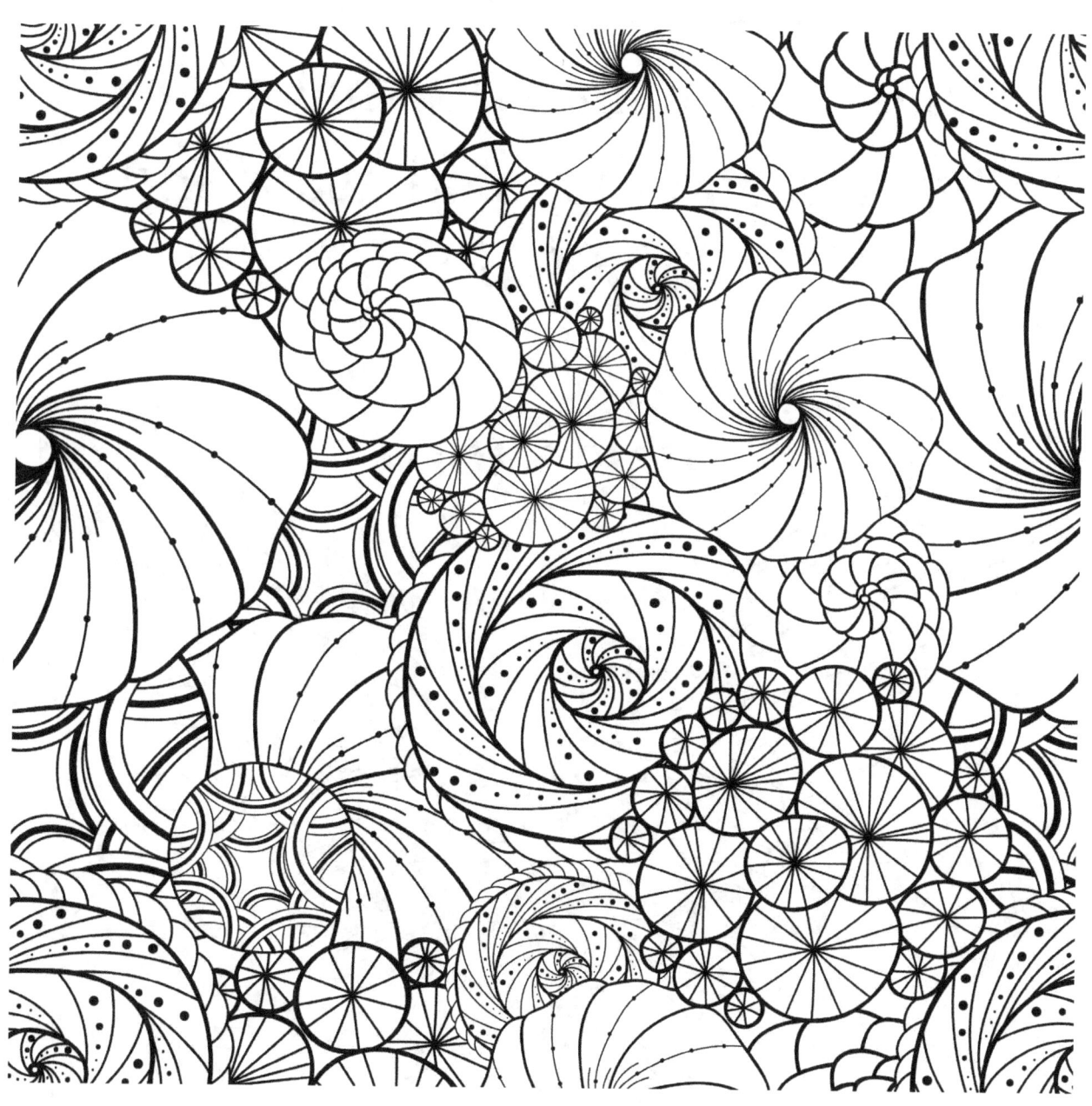

But they that wait upon the Lord shall renew their strength; they shall mount up with wings as eagles, they shall run and not be weary, and they shall walk and not faint.

Isaiah 40:31

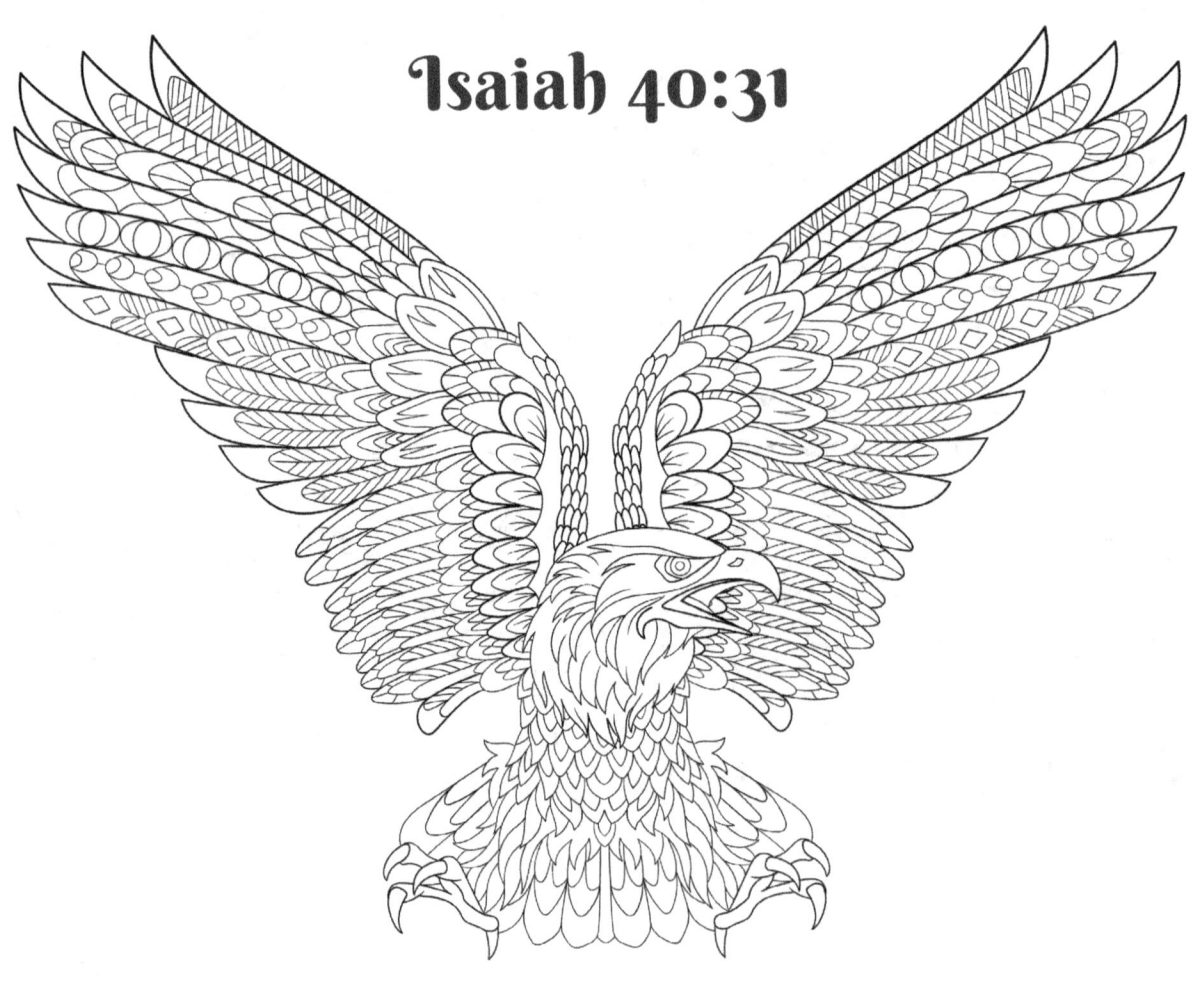

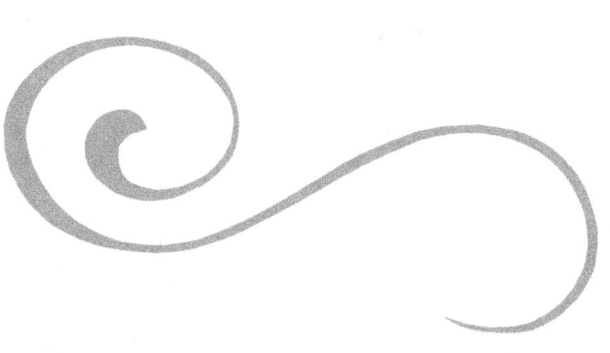

For God so loved the world that he gave his one and only Son, that whoever believes in him shall not perish but have eternal life.

John 3:16

Psalms 139:14
I will confess and praise You for You are fearful and wonderful and for the awful wonder of my birth! Wonderful are Your works, and that my inner self knows right well.

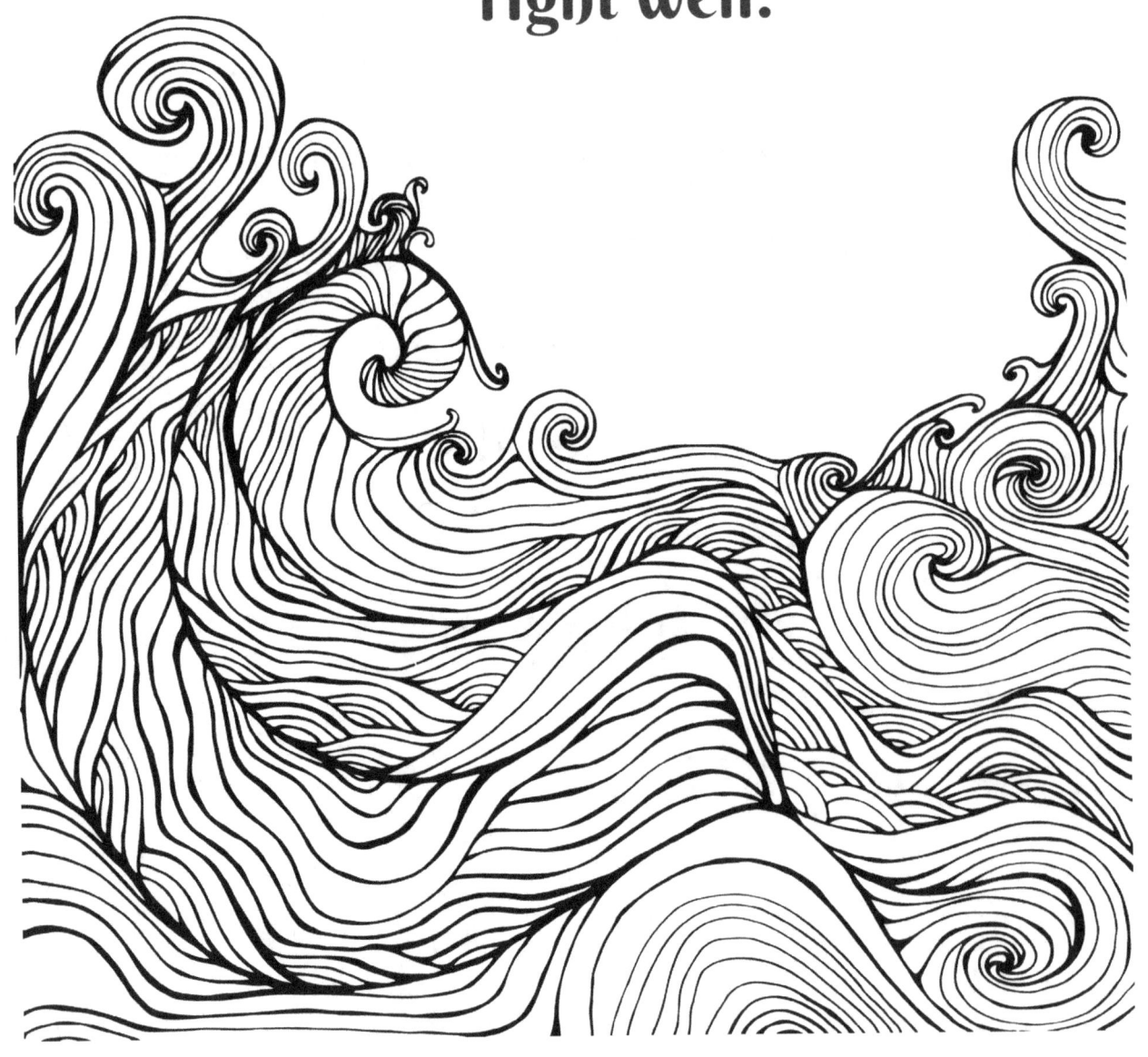

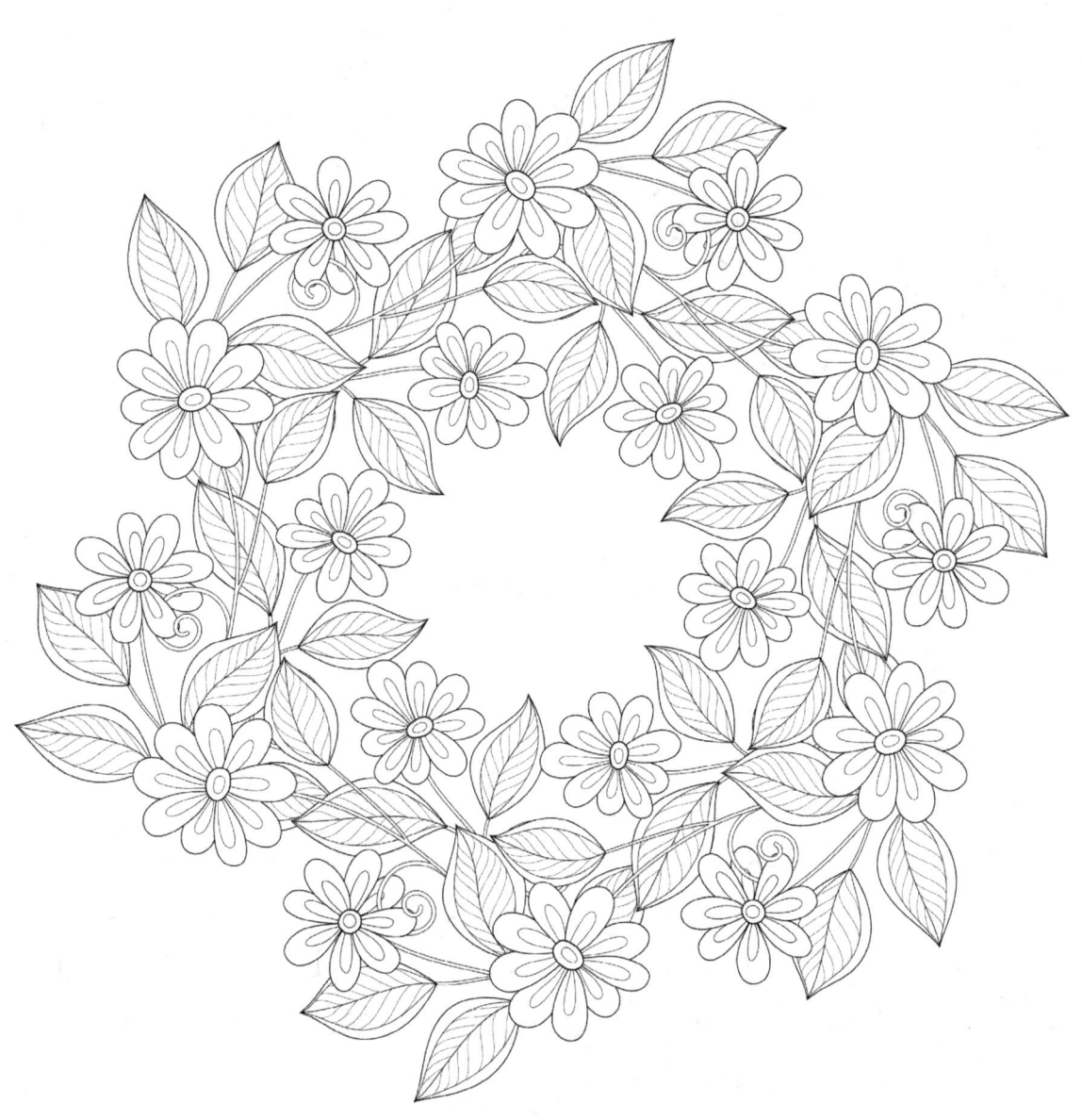

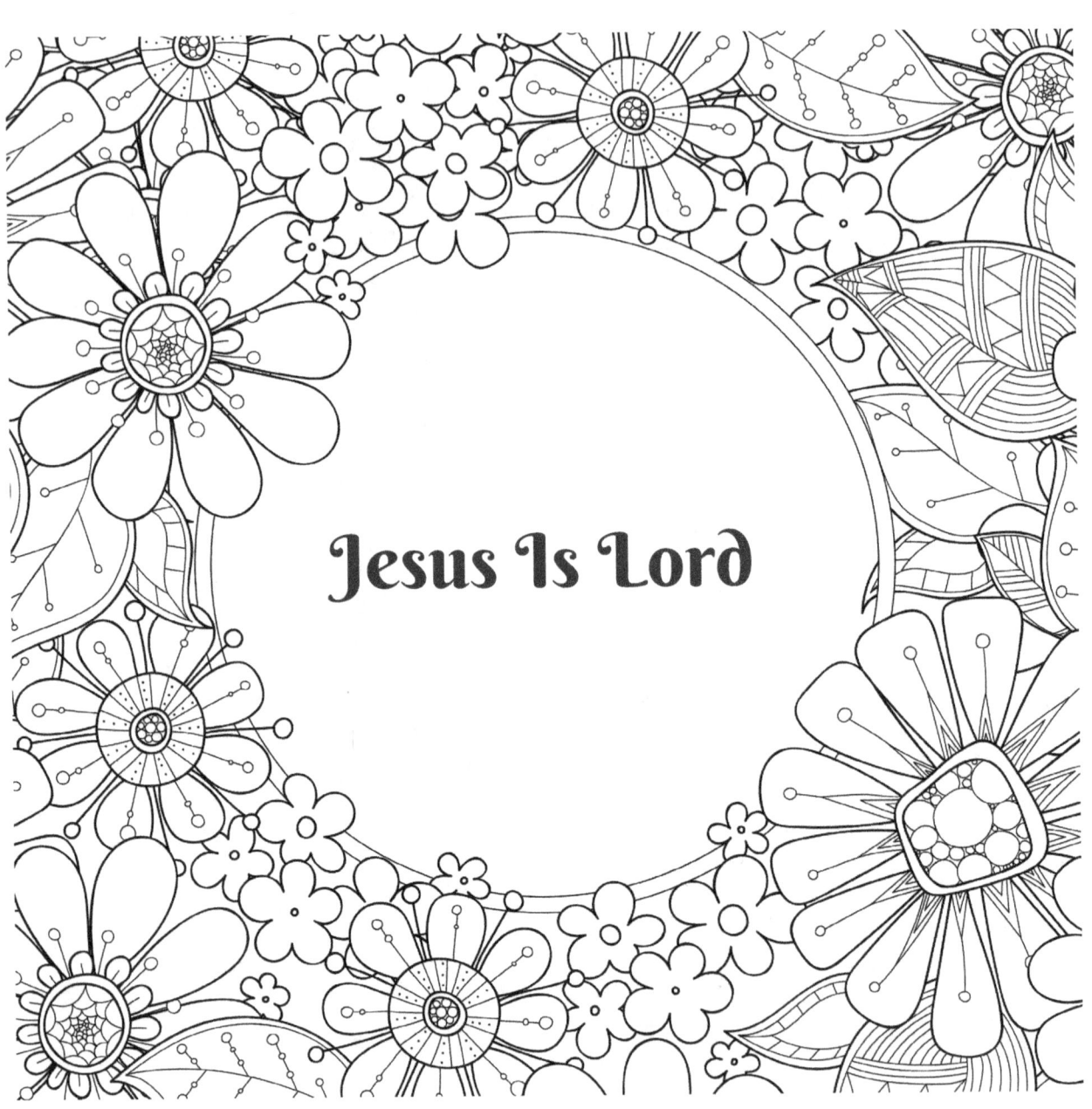

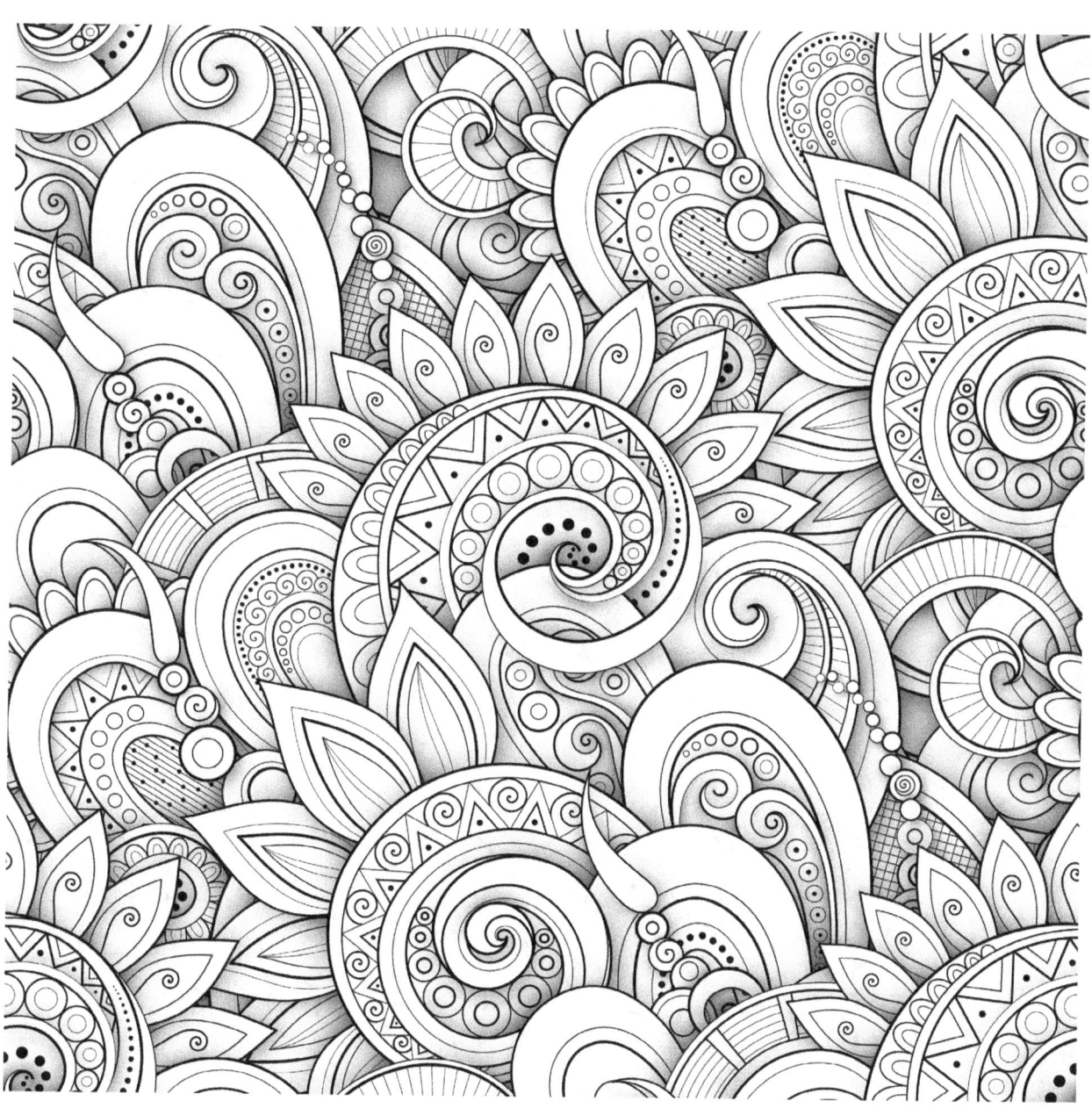

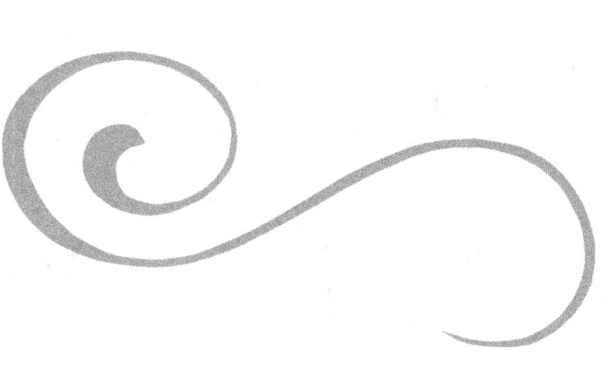

Therefore I tell you, whatever you ask for in prayer, believe that you have received it, and it will be yours.

Mark 11:24

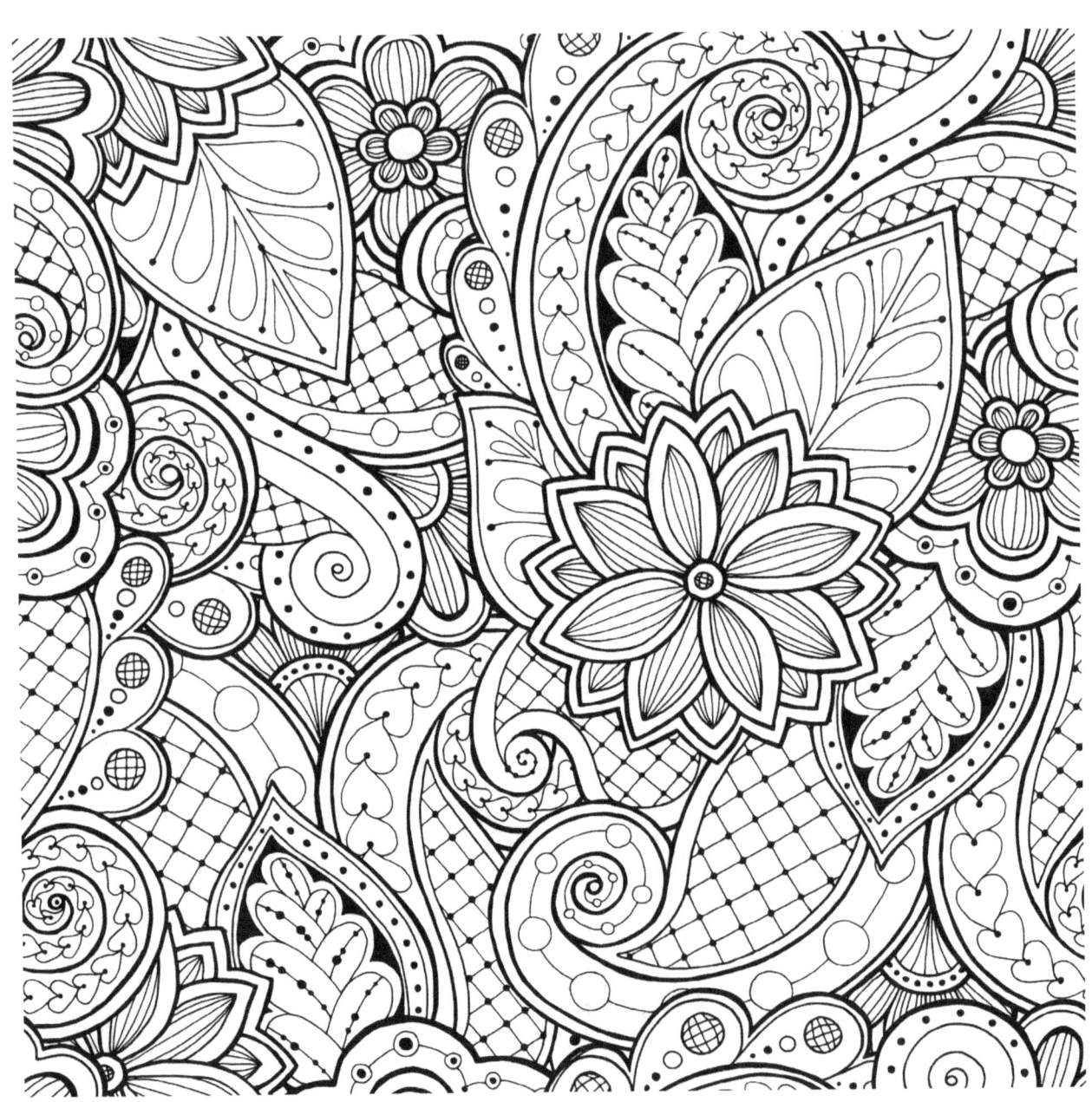

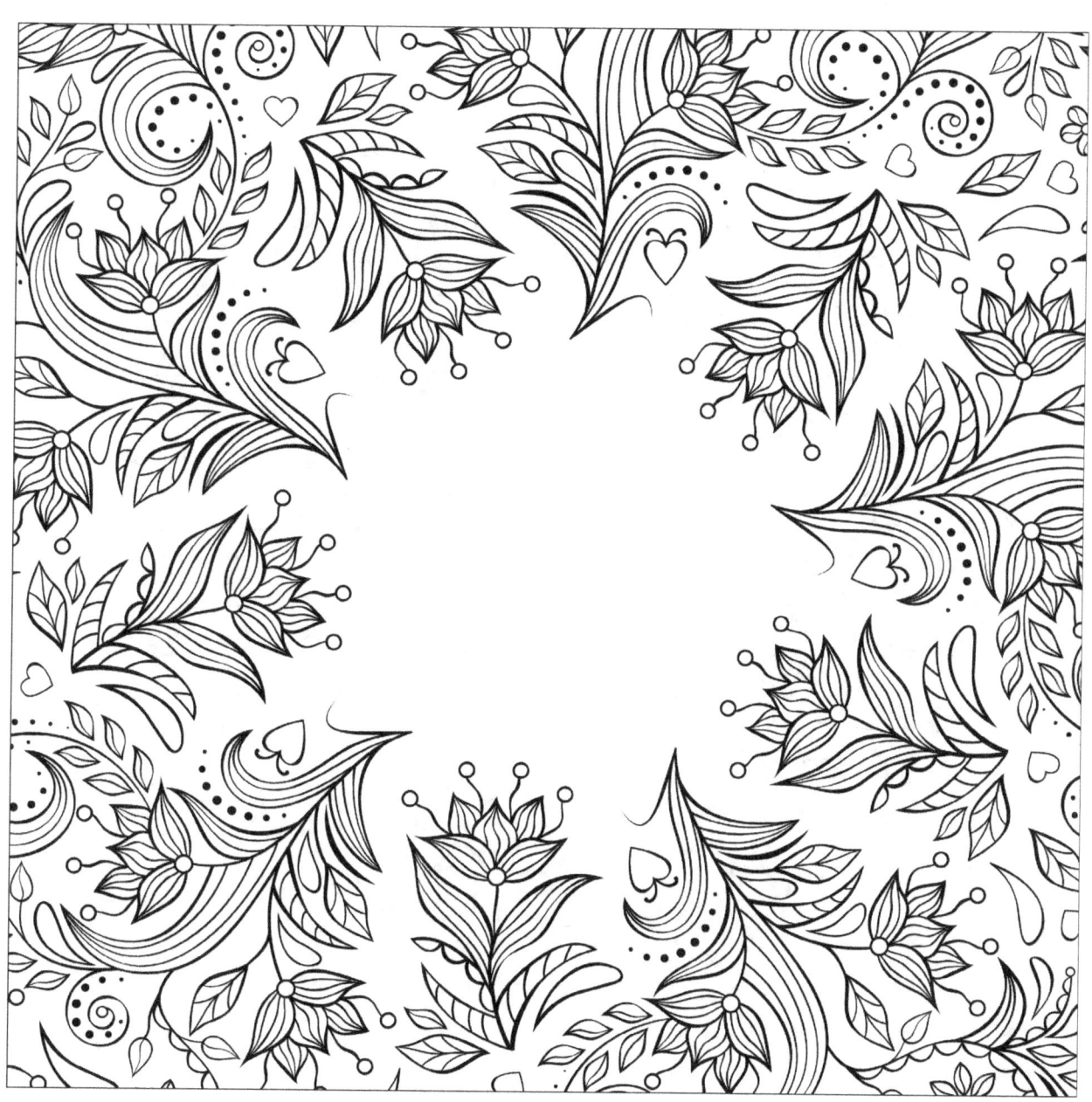

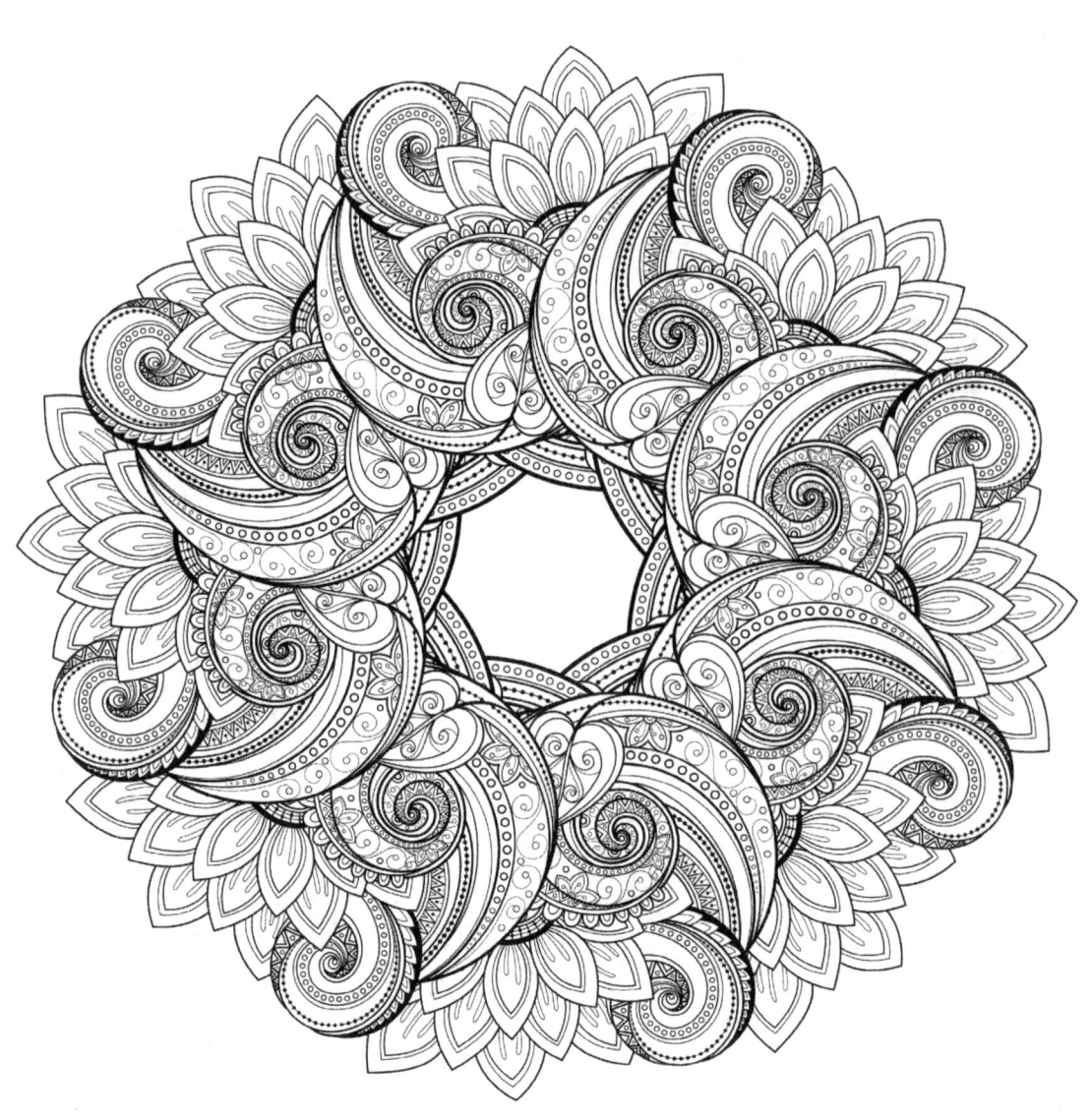

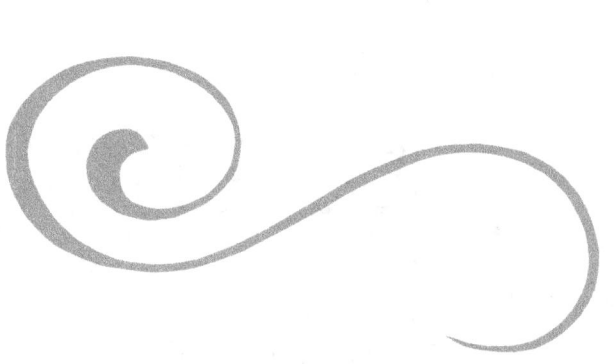

Take delight in the LORD, and he will give you the desires of your heart.

Psalms 37:4

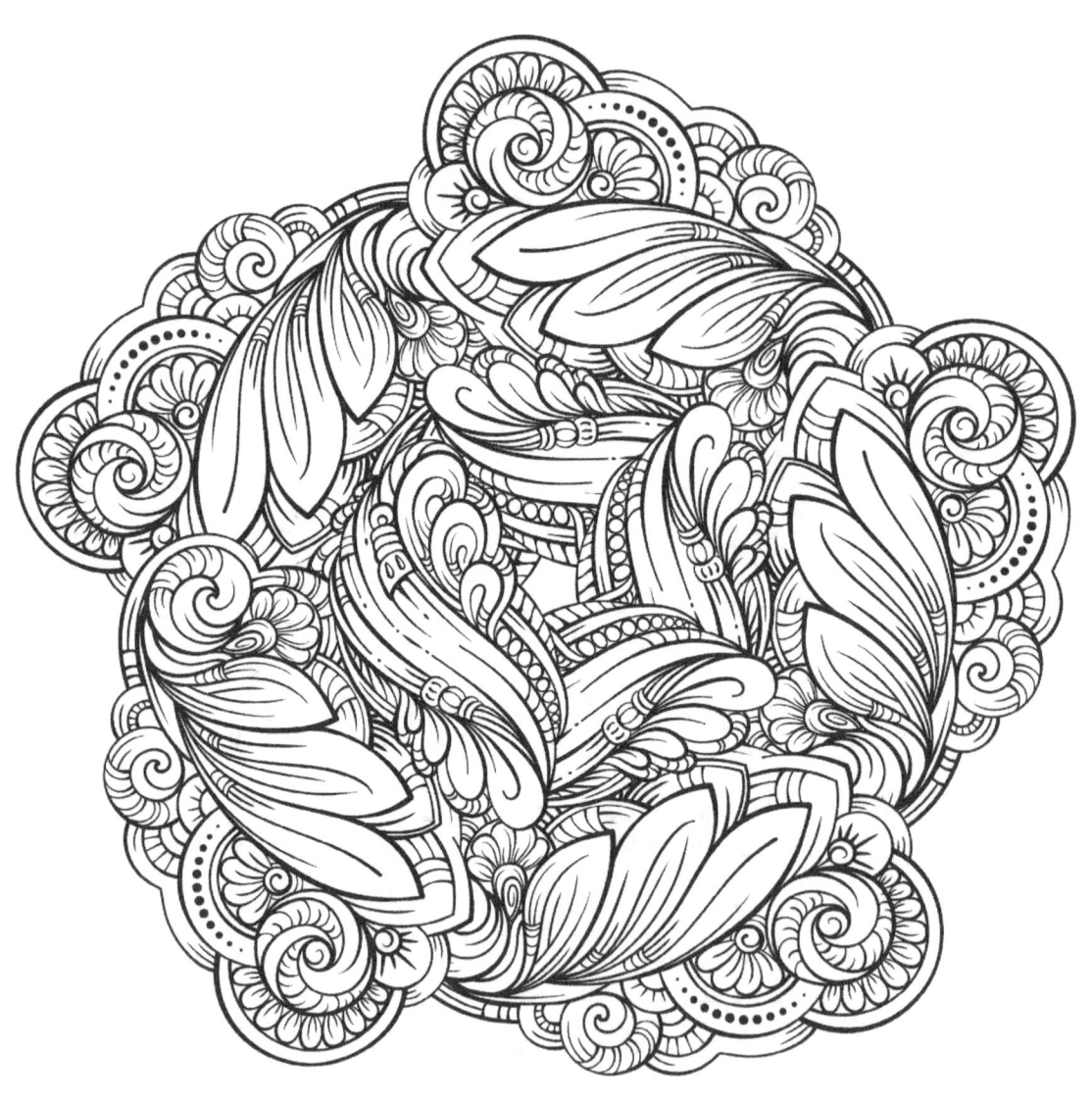

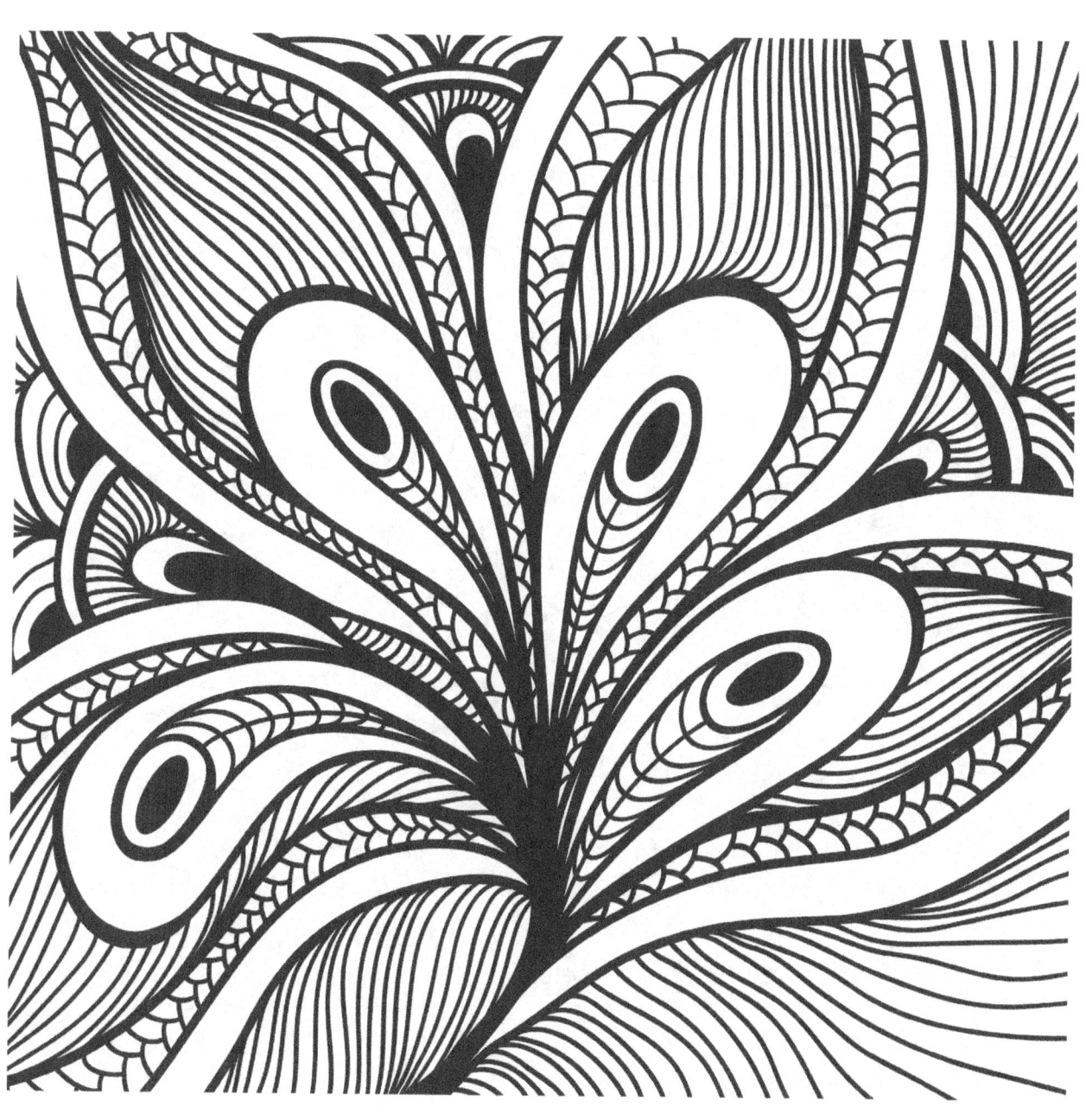

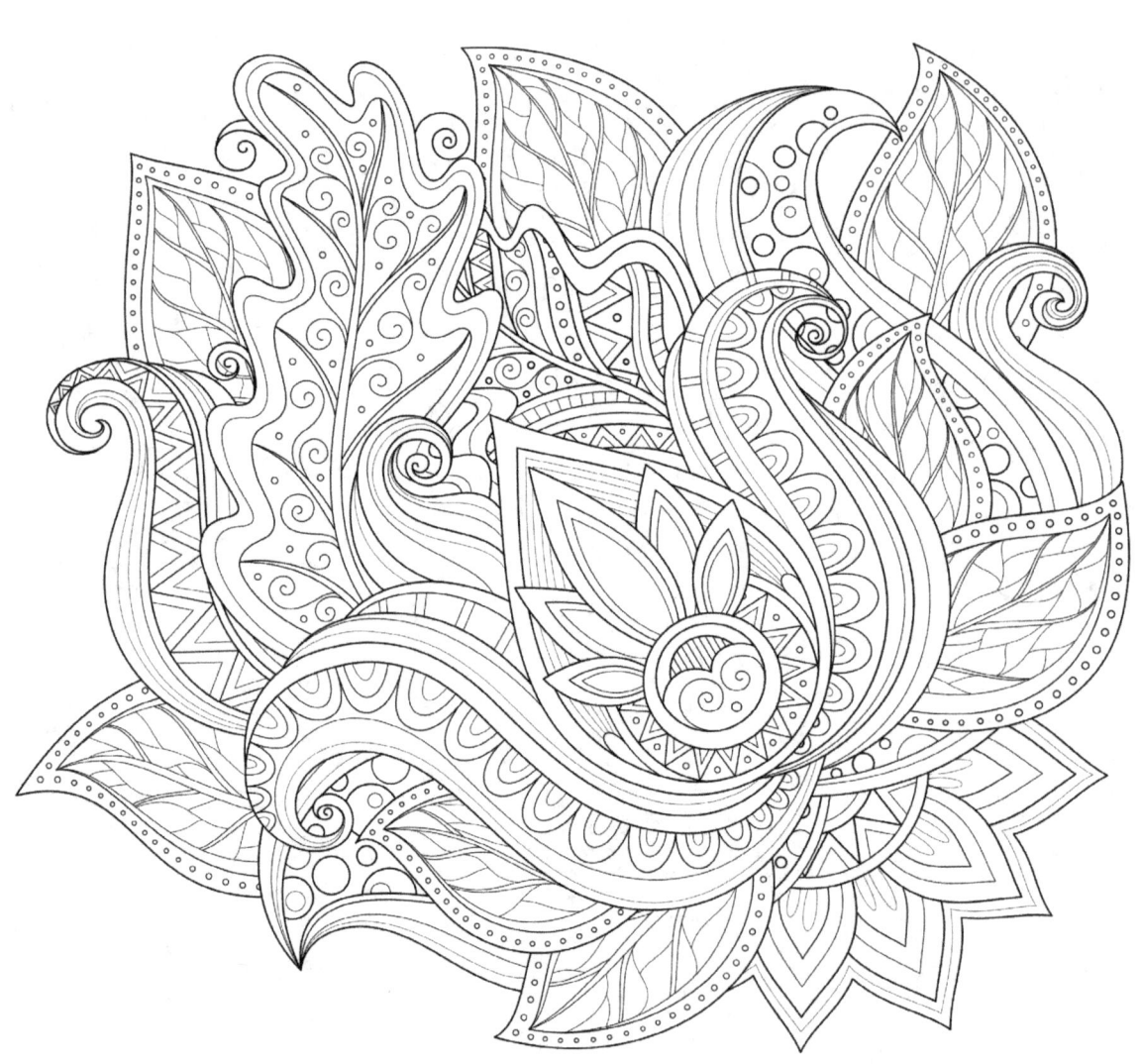

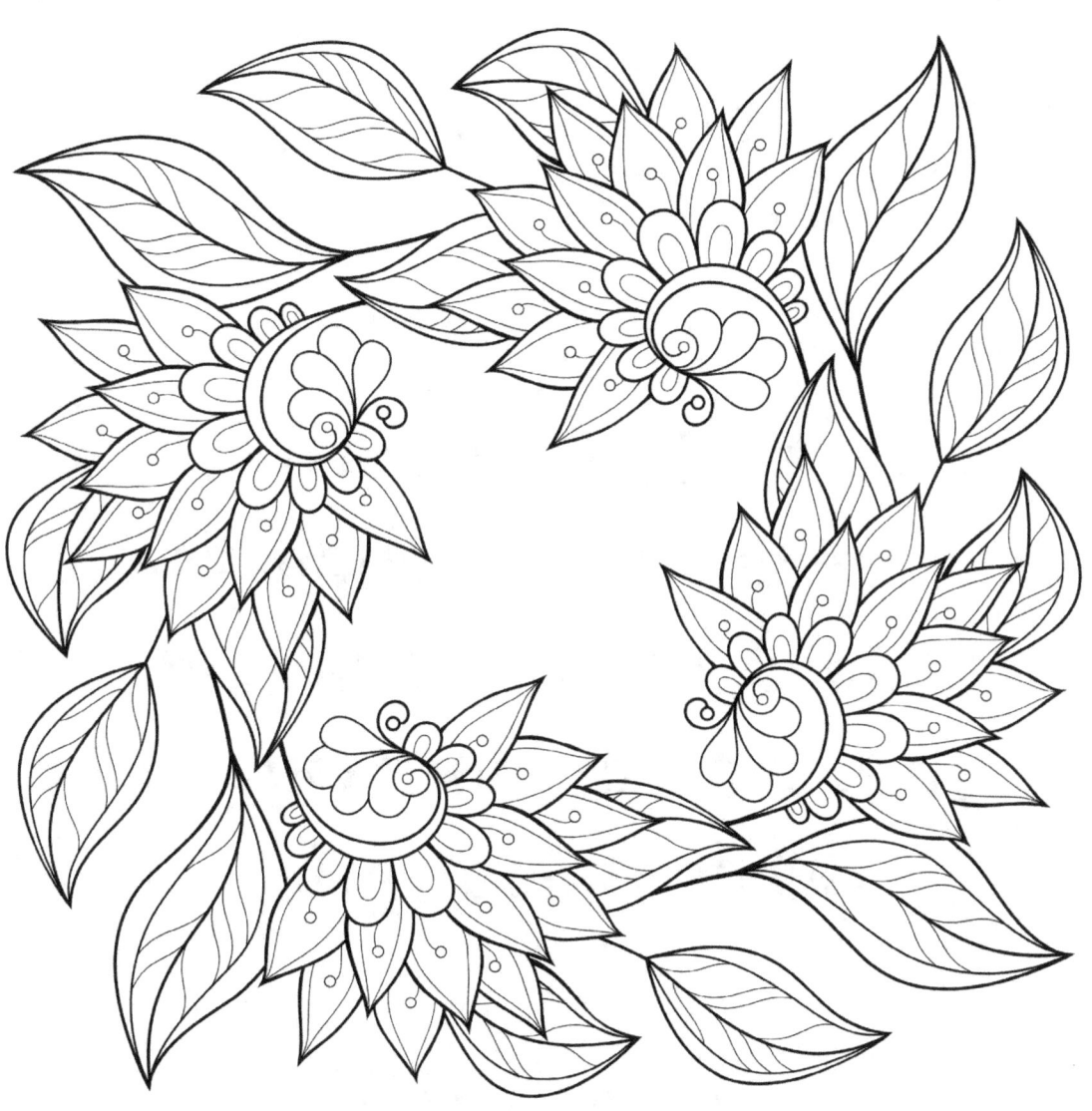

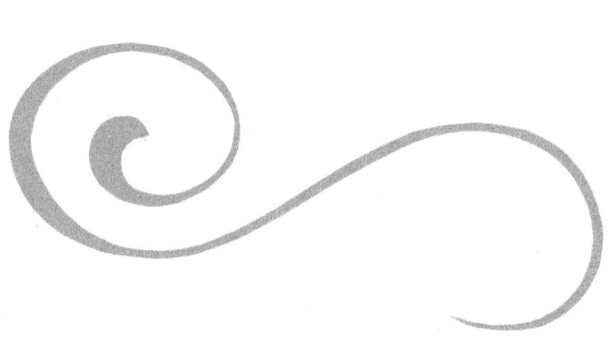

In Him we have redemption through his blood, the forgiveness of sins, in accordance with the riches of God's grace.

Ephesians 1:7

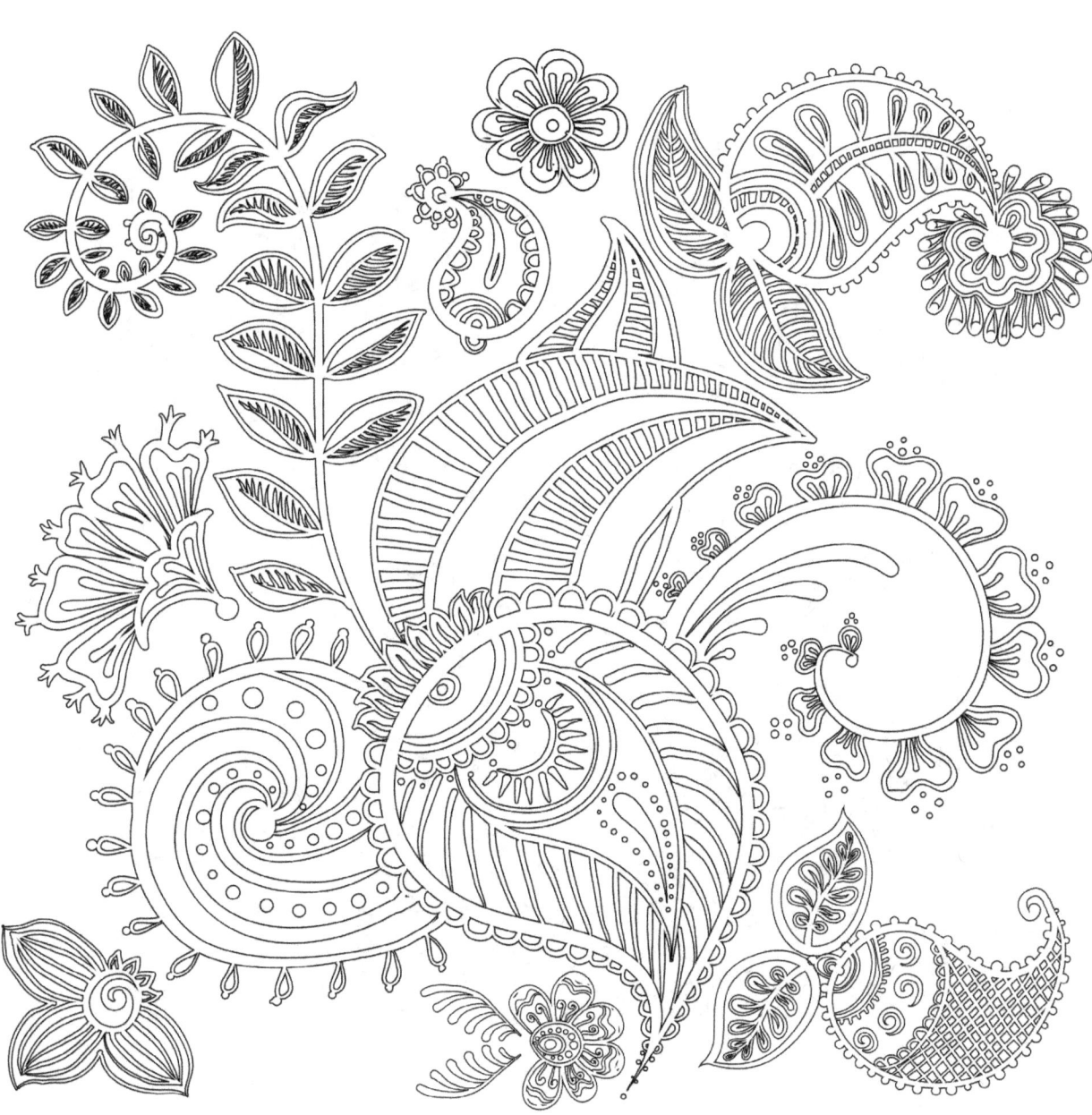

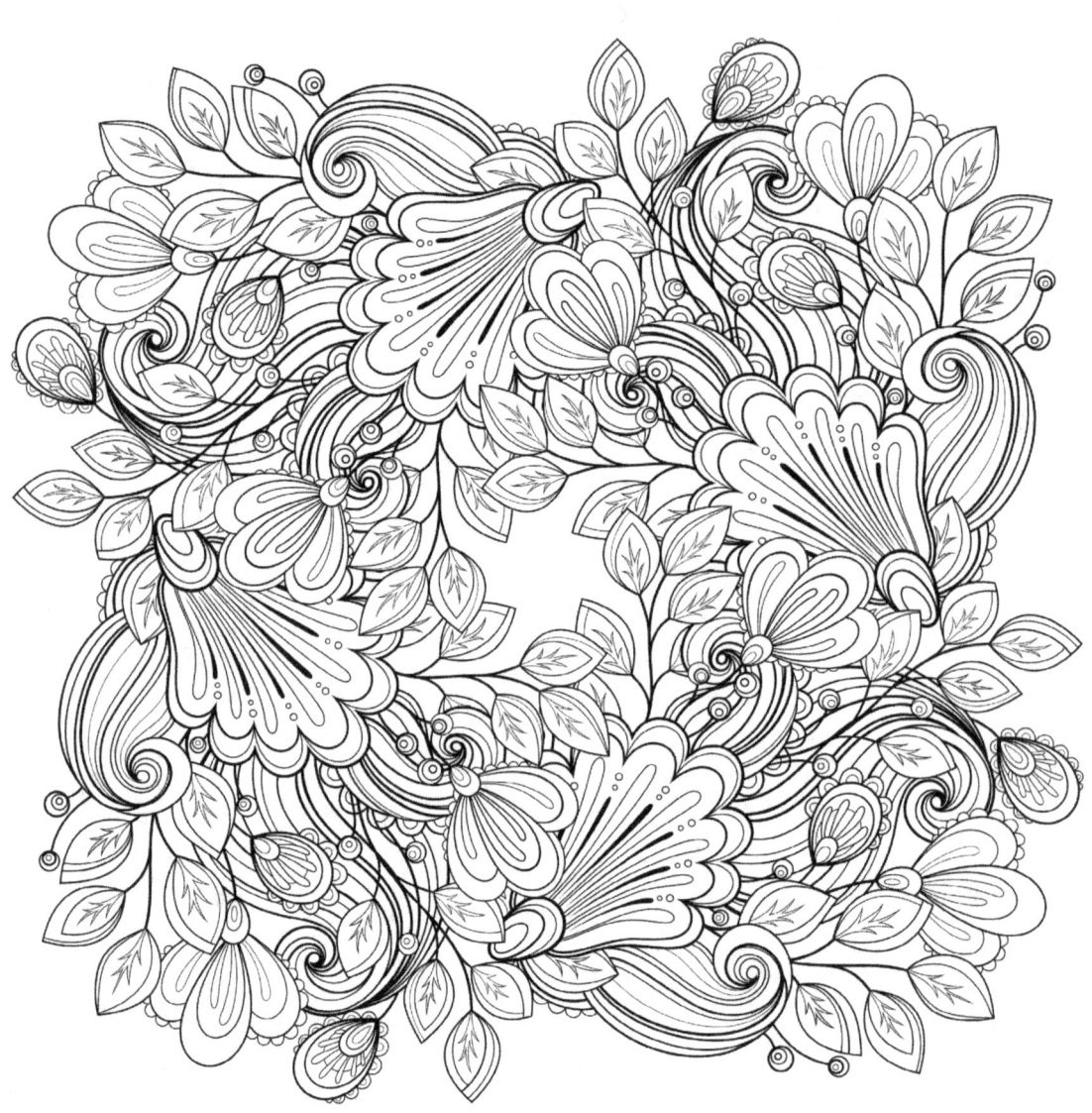

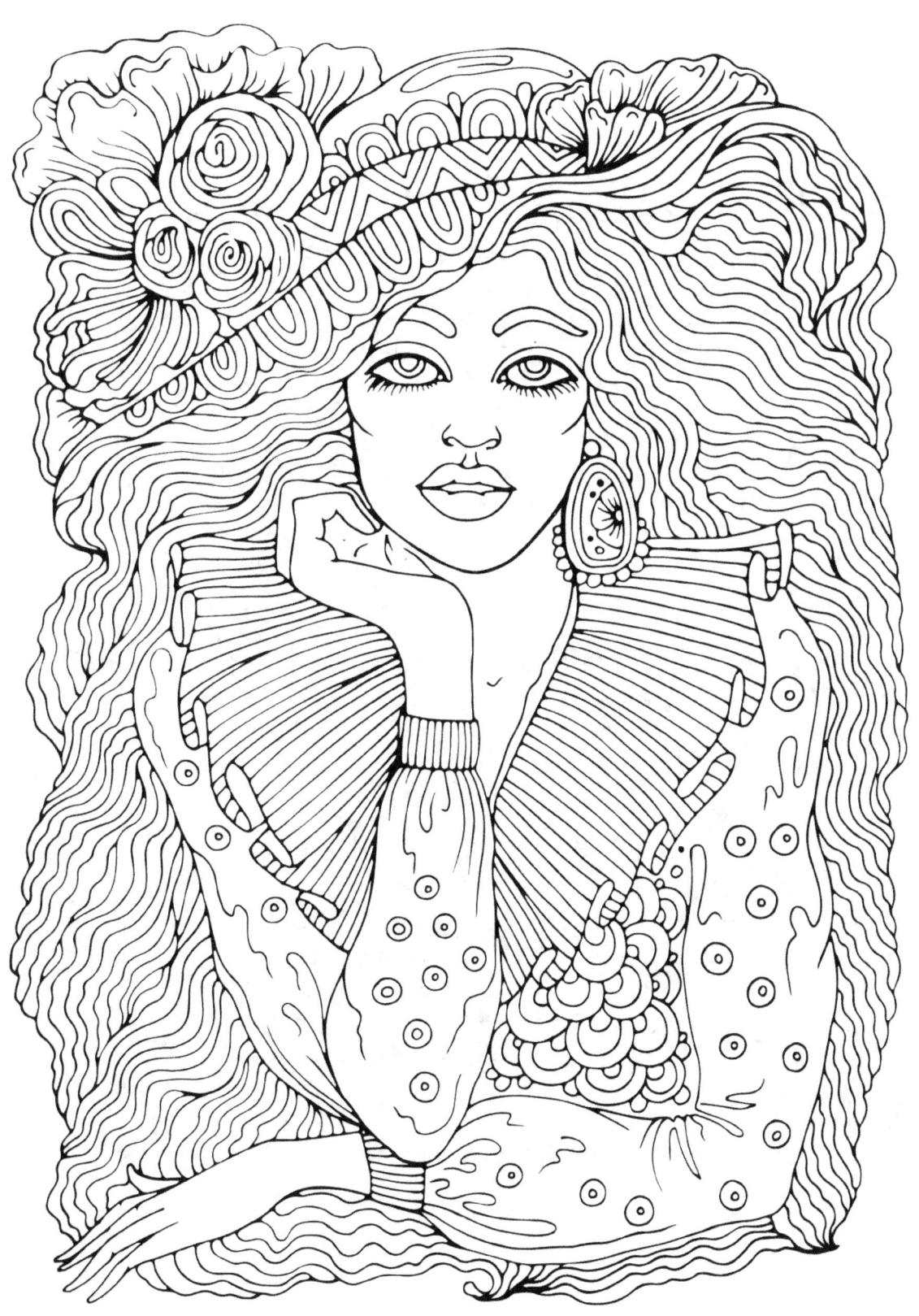

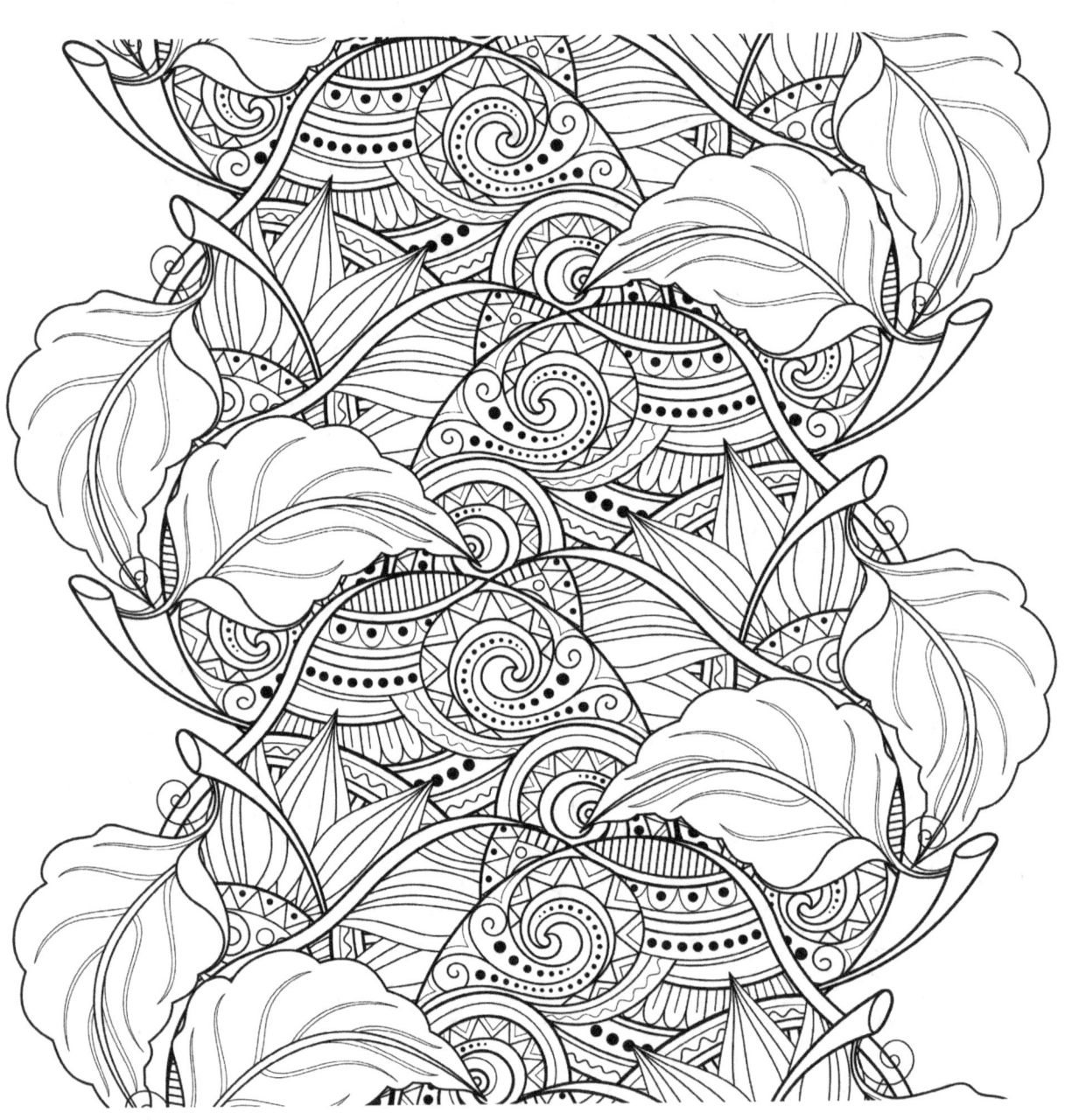

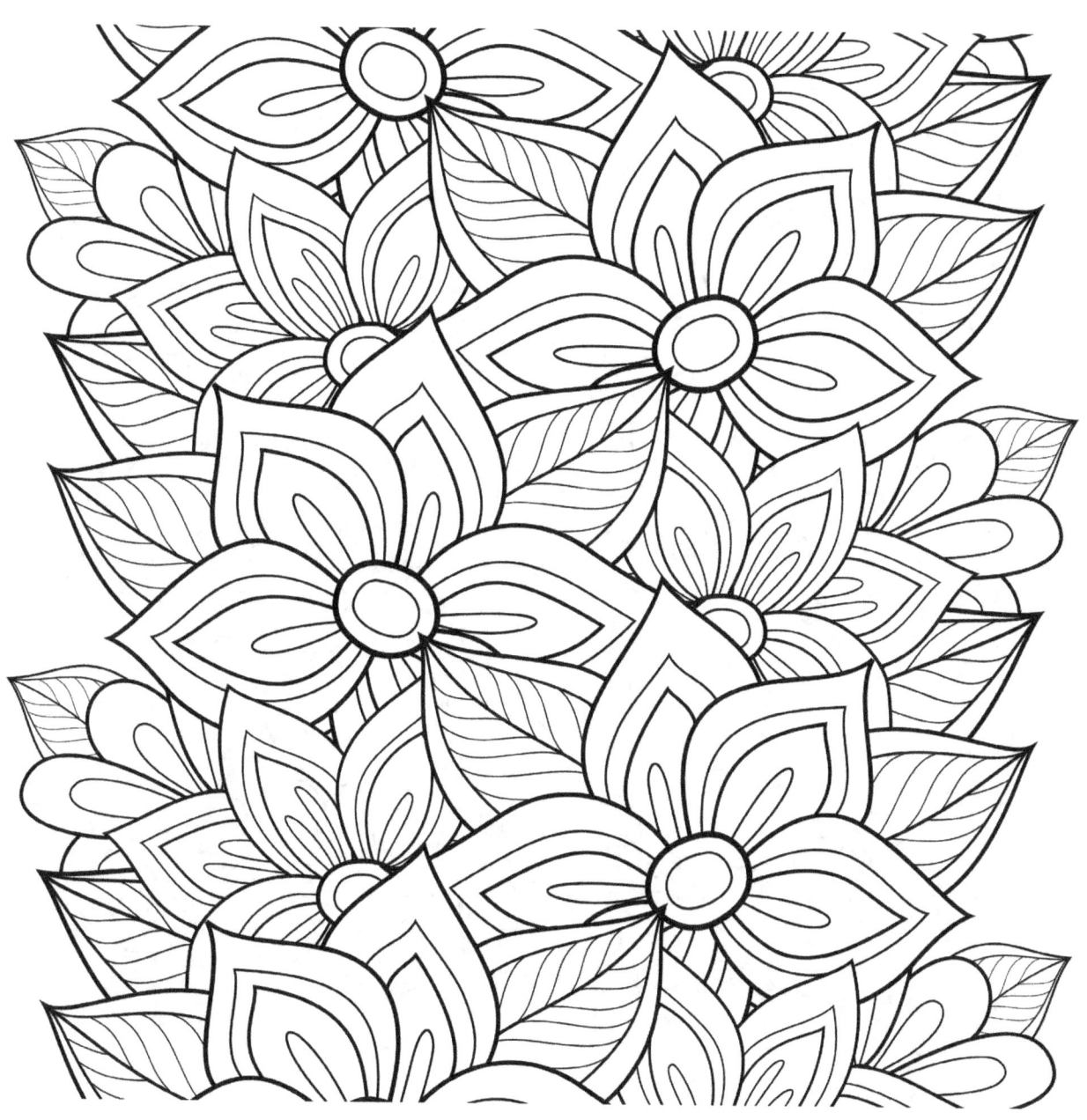

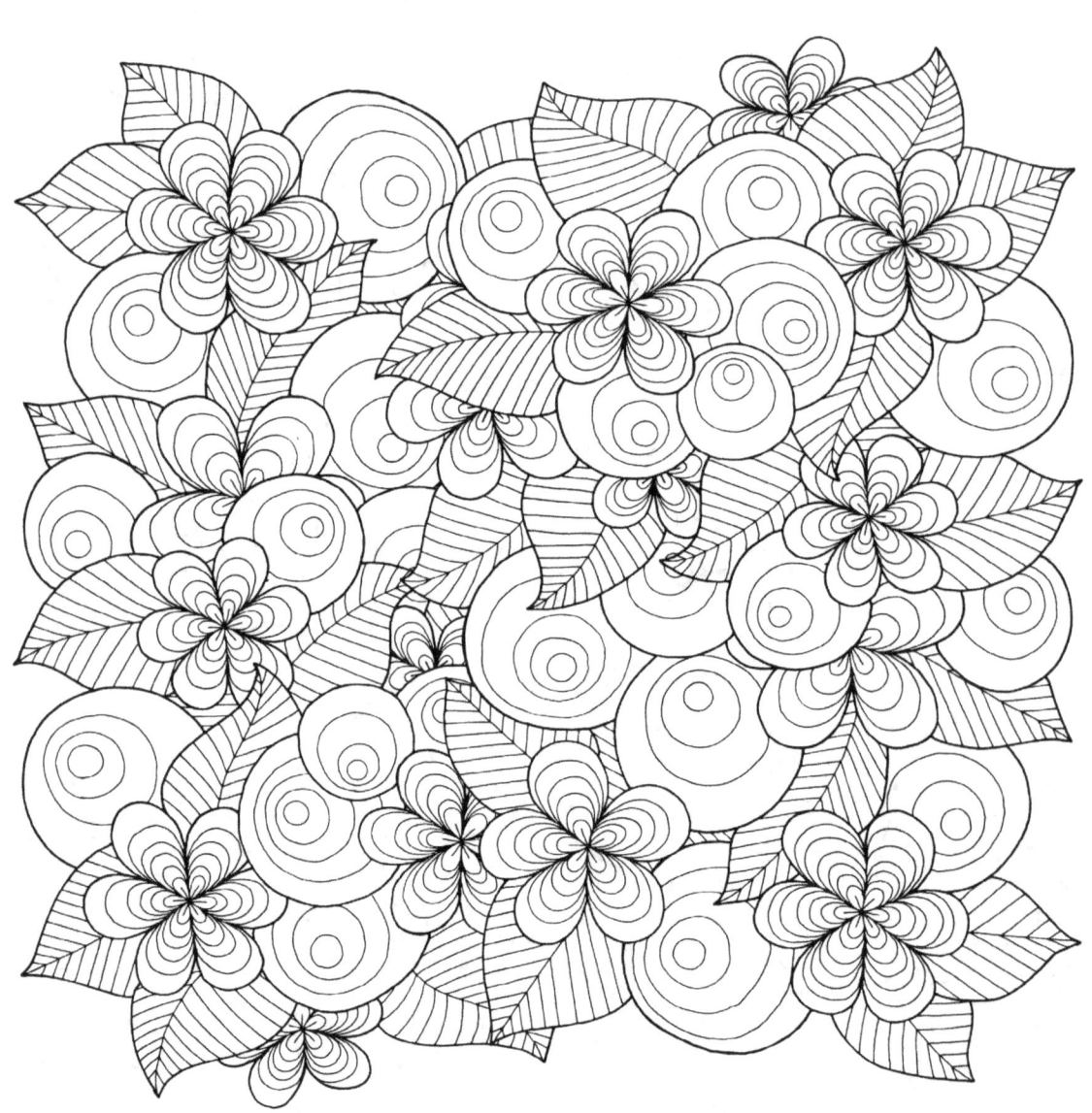

Book Reviews
****

Did you enjoy Scriptures in Color? Please consider writing a book review on Amazon, Barnes & Noble and Goodreads.

Book reviews are important to authors and it only takes a few minutes to write one.
A review doesn't have to be long.
A few short sentences or
a few words to describe the book works just fine.

Please join my mailing list for updates on events and future book releases.
www.pauletteharper.com

Thank you so much!!

Other Books by Paulette Harper

Secret Place Revealed~ 2017
Emma Award Winner, Best Fiction
Spiritual/Romance

Living Separate Lives

That Was Then, This Is Now

Faith for Every Mountain

Completely Whole

Princess Nevaeh: Lessons on Self-Discovery

www.ingramcontent.com/pod-product-compliance
Lightning Source LLC
Chambersburg PA
CBHW081019240526
45471CB00017B/3418